"Imagine applying the most powerful market segmentation strategy to every pricing transaction—the result is stealth execution that maximizes profitability. Jim Vaughn's **Stop Racing in a Blindfold!** is a must-read for business executives!"

Randy R. Brown
Chief Commercial Officer
Vortex Doors

"To consistently win at the racetrack, professional drivers have learned how to expand their visual fields. They don't focus on where they are, but where they want to be. Jim Vaughn's book, **Stop Racing in a Blindfold!**, is an excellent primer for executives to expand their visual fields by understanding the fundamentals of winning in a hyper-competitive marketplace. If you follow the principles within this book, you will consistently win customers, beat competitors, and get where you want to go."

Robert G. Cross
Chairman Emeritus
Revenue Analytics, Inc.

Author of NY Times Business Best Seller *Revenue Management: Hard Core Tactics for Market Domination*

"Jim Vaughn's book, **Stop Racing in a Blindfold!** bridges several complex topics in an accessible and engaging way. He provides practical advice for how big data and modern pricing science techniques can unlock value in a wide range of businesses. For executives who want to stay ahead in competitive business environments, this is required reading!"

Stephen Moss, Ph.D.
Former McKinsey & Company Partner

Praise for *Stop Racing In A Blindfold!*

"Pricing is one of the highest impact decisions within most businesses, yet one of the least understood. Jim Vaughn's book is the best starting point I know for companies pricing in Business-to-Business markets to improve profits using pricing science. I highly recommend it to any executive who wants to understand how they can gain a critical edge in the competitive race through more targeted pricing and thereby stop 'leaving fuel on the track.'"

Robert Phillips, Ph.D.
Former Director, Pricing Research, Amazon
Former Director Marketplace Optimization Data Sciences
Founder & Chief Science Officer, Nomis Solutions
Founder & CEO Decision Focus

Author of *Pricing and Revenue Optimization*, Stanford University Press
Co-editor of the *Oxford Handbook of Pricing Management*, Oxford University Press

"Stop Racing in a Blindfold! illustrates for **a senior exec audience** how to apply pricing theory to address practical, real-world problems. If this book's ideas and tools are not a part of your sales and pricing strategies, you are definitely leaving money on the table. From someone long involved in analytics and data driven decision making, Jim Vaughn's new book was a great intro into a new domain. I can easily see how it would have great impact on a healthy business or a turn-around opportunity."

Walter J Muller III, Ph. D.
Former Chief Investment Officer
Bank of America

"Execs always talk about 'taking care of the customer' and creating a 'win-win' to drive profitable sales. In Jim Vaughn's new book, he shows how this is practical. By understanding each customer's willingness to pay, companies can price their products in a market-aware range that sales reps and their customers can enthusiastically support."

Robert Mraz
Vice President, Sales & Marketing
TW Metals, Inc.

Praise for *Stop Racing In A Blindfold!*

"Jim Vaughn's book, **Stop Racing in a Blindfold!**, provides a terrific introduction to, and compelling examples of, the key ideas used to extract valuable and actionable insights from data in the complex domain of B2B pricing. Some of these are: the power of using imperfect, but helpful, models; segmenting transactions, not customers; pricing attributes when products are unique; and using 'differences-in-differences' to accurately measure the impact of better pricing. **I highly recommend this book to executives of B2B companies who are looking for practical ways to leverage the power of data science to drive high-impact performance improvement.**"

Loren Williams, Ph.D.
Former Chief Data Scientist
Global Analytics, EY

"With **Stop Racing in a Blindfold!**, Jim Vaughn has bridged the longstanding gap between pricing theory and the practical application of pricing science with straightforward explanations and examples. This book will be recommended reading for all of our P&L owners and required reading for our pricing team."

Bob Vezeau
Former Vice President, Strategic Pricing
Corrugated Packaging Solutions, WestRock

"As said in the movie Jerry Maguire, 'Show Me the Money.' Jim puts it out there in simple examples. Whether you are a senior exec, a sales manager, or a pricing manager, you can find the steps to change the race and make a huge impact on your company. There is no winner's circle without pricing analytics and the right optimization tools."

Al Payne
Former CEO
WebOps - A medical device logistics and analytics company

Praise for *Stop Racing In A Blindfold!*

"Board Members, VCs, CXOs and sales leaders should read this book. There's a lot to learn! Business leadership is about understanding new opportunities to create a market advantage, setting the direction, and enabling a team to make it happen. Jim Vaughn's book **Stop Racing in a Blindfold!** shows how it's very possible to create a market advantage from data businesses already have. Gaining this insight will prevent both lost sales and money left on the table—a game changer."

F. Scott Tuck
Member, Board of Directors, BlackRidge Technology
Advisory Board Member & North American Fund Director, Silk Invest Limited
Advisory Board Member & Fund Director ValueQuest Asset Management
Senior Advisor and Partner, Ascent Investment Partners
Formerly CEO and CMO, Montgomery Asset Management
West Point Graduate and former Special Ops Aviator

Stop Racing in a Blindfold!
Big Data + Pricing Science Drive Bigger Profits

Stop Racing in a Blindfold!
Big Data + Pricing Science
Drive Bigger Profits

Jim Vaughn

University Training Partners Publishing

Publication Data
Vaughn, James E.
Stop racing in a blindfold! big data + pricing science
drive bigger profits / Jim Vaughn
p. cm.
ISBN 978-0-9906838-6-5
1. Pricing Science 2. Business to Business Pricing 3. Economics 4. Pricing Analytics
I. Vaughn, James E. II. Title.

First Printing: June 2015
Second Edition: February 2024

Book Cover by Caroline Vaughn

University Training Partners Publishing
Fair Oaks, CA 95628
www.UTP-US.com

Dedication

To my mother, who always encouraged my curiosity and hard work. Thank you Mom! And, to my wife and children for their patience while I spent many hours of family time on this book.

Contents

Table of Illustrations

Acknowledgments

Thanks especially go to Mary, my wife of over 30 years. A fellow consultant and expert statistician, Dr. Mary McShane-Vaughn helped many times in many ways to bring this book to fruition with reviews and suggestions to improve the content and readability. This book would not have been possible without her constant support in the initial effort and this 2024 revision.

Additionally, this book has immeasurably benefitted from years of conversations and experience involving both clients and colleagues. Without the benefits of those experiences, this book would not have been remotely possible. So, to my many friends, if you see a story in here that reminds you of some exchange or event, please know I am very appreciative of the insights I have gained. In addition, several of my colleagues provided invaluable assistance in reviewing this book and providing significant suggestions that also greatly improved the readability and completeness of this book. For that help, my sincere appreciation goes to: Barrett Thompson, Brooks Hamilton, John O'Connor, Dr. Hosam Zaki, Lindsay Duran and Rich Flati for their focused comments…Thank You!

Preface to the Second Edition

To you, the reader, I truly appreciate your interest in this update.

So why am I updating my book after eight years? Did the principles of how to "price smarter" change? No. So, what's new in the world of pricing excellence that warrants devoting time to put out a new edition on the core elements of segmentation, optimization, and pricing? <u>Mainly, it is mindset and opportunity</u>. Companies have learned a lot since 2015. Capabilities have grown a lot. Part of that change in mindset is also a hugely different way to sell. Many B2B businesses are rethinking their value to the customer and moving to service-based pricing. Software licensing has been doing this for a long time, but a larger number of B2B businesses in fields as diverse as jet engines, truck tires and infrastructure have moved some or all of their business to a subscription model. This brings greater predictability to suppliers and customers, but <u>it also means thinking about pricing in new ways</u>. And ultimately, it helps align value with our customers and it reinforces the customer's lifetime value. See Danilo Zatta's book The Pricing Model Revolution.

In terms of pricing solutions, we are now in a rapid growth stage; we are no longer talking about early adopter companies using 'AI/ML' (artificial intelligence / machine learning) and pricing science. Since I started in the pricing field thirty-plus years ago, I've repeatedly heard from Gartner, IDC and other research consultancies, "pricing, it's the next big thing!" **The future has arrived.** And with it, some loose talk.

People very extensively use the term 'data science' to imply specific knowledge to address pricing tasks. But *data science is just a technical skill set* that can be used in pricing science. The buzz label AI/ML is bandied about, implying knowledge to address pricing. But 'data science' and 'AI/ML' capabilities are very broad—far more than just pricing. They include capabilities in natural language processing, visual/optical processing, neural networks, and just general patterning capabilities—<u>some</u> of these techniques can be used in pricing science.

The biggest reason why 'the future has arrived!' is that today's B2C and B2B business leaders are more experienced in dealing with volatile markets and have <u>accepted</u> that prices can be changed as market conditions change over relatively shorter periods of time. What we collectively experienced over the last three to four years has changed us. It changed our markets, and it changed our customers.

- Since the release of this book in 2015, global markets have moved from low inflation to essentially no inflation, to the highest inflation in 40 years, and today both demand and costs are rather more stable, at least for now.
  - Supply chains have generally worked their way back to normalcy or at least to a steadier steady state.
  - Demand has softened for certain types of goods. Whether demand steadies or heats up again, the problem is how and where does a business respond to both ups and downs, and by how much?
- Because B2B and B2C Customers have experienced the full gamut of price changes in a relatively short period, there is a lot that business has learned.
- The pandemic brought many business challenges. Every business hunkered down initially.
  - Some businesses twisted their delivery model and completely reinvented themselves.
  - Others were defensive and then saw demand grow explosively, followed by explosive cost increases while supply chains struggled to adapt.
- In late 2022 and early 2023 we began to see something quite different. As an example, ocean freight shipping container rates dropped about 90% from the pandemic level peaks, and this rippled through the economy.

Summing up the situation, I believe one of the biggest take-aways is that 'Econ 101' really is quite informative about the real world.
- When supply is constrained and demand goes up, customers who are willing to pay more will in fact pay more, and those that aren't so inclined will look for substitute products or services, or just do without.
- And when supply is less constrained, or demand gets soft the reverse happens.
- In short:
  - **When there is no demand,** your market price does not matter and there is no point in discounting (think of cruise lines?)
  - **When there is no supply,** your market price does not matter and there is no point in discounting (think of home appliances or cars during the pandemic?).

Here are two questions to consider:
- Can a business be in a defensive posture and an offensive posture at the same time? Yes, if you think in terms of customer type, product hierarchy, geography, and order details.

- When should a business go after margin rate vs. market share growth—how can a business use predictive analytics to better know what to expect, and to inform better decisions?

These questions can be answered directly with confidence by leveraging the capabilities of pricing science, leveraging AI/ML. These tools have been 'battle tested' over the last 40-plus years, and especially so since the first edition of 'Stop Racing in a Blindfold' in 2015.

What enabled some businesses to cope better with the market challenges of the last 4-5 years? Part of that answer is businesses have been grappling with a decades-long acceleration in the rate of change of business markets. As a result, many businesses pursued digital initiatives. Equally, if not more importantly, customer expectations changed as the world changed. Customers demanded more price transparency. Buyers pushed manufacturers / distributors / service providers to see the same price on their website as they expected from a handshake, or per a contract, or via the price list they buy from every day. Channel management, price list management, contract price management, and similar challenges got a lot of business leaders' attention. As a result of that focus, certain businesses found it easier to be more agile, while others struggled more, lacking in those advantages. Some even started to introduce service-based pricing (some would call this outcome-based pricing) and grappled with how they would price that.

What price management solution approaches were most valuable to many B2B and B2C businesses?
- Some businesses invested in better technology enablers.
- Some invested in price setting solutions, others in price management solutions.
- Some invested in better, more scalable business processes.
- Some invested in all.

The core question they asked was 'how can my business manage all these market and customer-facing demands and do so in a scalable (and hopefully flawless) manner?'

One key part of these solutions was better, closed-loop pricing analytics. It's a truism that you can't effectively manage what you can't see and measure. Another part of these price management improvements often involved adopting a more defined pricing framework, like the one in the next page, which organizes and structures 'pricing vehicles.'

A customer may have access to buy certain products through certain channels with specific T&Cs which allows the customer to access specific pricing. Having a well-defined pricing structure also makes it easier to have clearer standard pricing analytics reports available.

The chart below reflects a well-established framework for managing List Prices, website/internet prices, tier/matrix/schedule price levels, agreement/contract prices, and one-time/spot market/override or special/project prices. Beyond a better framework for managing prices, what else did some of those businesses do? Many leveraged pricing science to keep their prices aligned and updated with much less manual effort. All these steps provided key agility in the market at critical junctures in the pandemic and post-pandemic years.

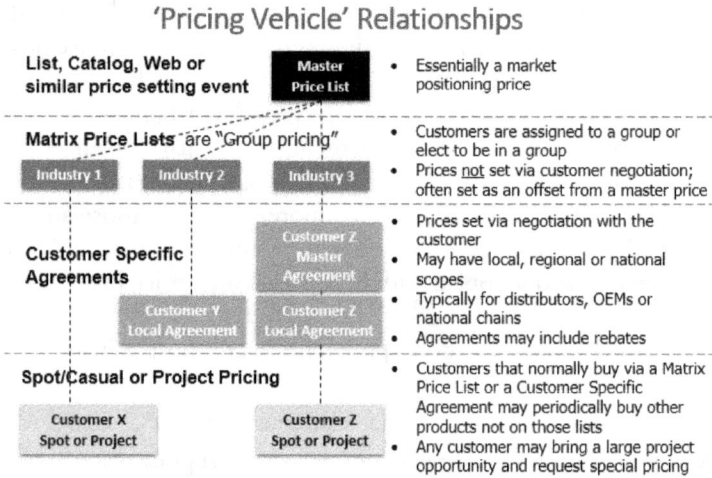

'Pricing Vehicle' Relationships

List, Catalog, Web or similar price setting event	**Master Price List**	•	Essentially a market positioning price
Matrix Price Lists are "Group pricing"		•	Customers are assigned to a group or elect to be in a group
Industry 1 / Industry 2 / Industry 3		•	Prices not set via customer negotiation; often set as an offset from a master price
Customer Specific Agreements	Customer Z Master Agreement	•	Prices set via negotiation with the customer
		•	May have local, regional or national scopes
Customer Y Local Agreement	Customer Z Local Agreement	•	Typically for distributors, OEMs or national chains
		•	Agreements may include rebates
Spot/Casual or Project Pricing		•	Customers that normally buy via a Matrix Price List or a Customer Specific Agreement may periodically buy other products not on those lists
Customer X Spot or Project	Customer Z Spot or Project	•	Any customer may bring a large project opportunity and request special pricing

But maybe you are in the sceptic camp. Are you thinking this pricing science 'hooey' is just pie-in-the-sky noise when it comes to your company's business? It just can't solve your business' pricing challenges because your pricing is just too complex. There's too much nuance. If you are in that camp, or sitting on the fence, you are wondering why some pundits assert pricing science is our salvation, and some business leaders say it can't solve 'my' problems.

Where is the gap in perspectives? I believe fundamentally the gap is that the two groups are talking about two different future state visions.
- Group A: is the "AI/ML doubter" group.
- Group B: is the "Help sales sell smarter" group.

Group A will imply one of the main objectives of pricing science is to replace the sales rep with a 'machine' and then assert it's simply not possible.

Group B will ask if pricing science can help leave less money on the table.

I'm in Group B because I've been doing this for 30-plus years and know the possibilities are real. But I agree with Group A, you cannot replace the Sales team with a 'machine.'

Ask any group of Sales Reps what's a "good price" for a product, and there will be at least as many answers as there are sales reps and customers they sell to. Good Sales Reps think about each customer and their specific prices and the value/fit of that product to that customer's use—value-based pricing.

- What alternatives does a customer have?
- How good a fit is my product for my customer's needs?
- What is the quality/brand reputation of my product?
- How good/reliable is my customer service?
- How easy does my customer think I am to do business with? (market agility/speed, accuracy of billing, customer/technical support, payment terms, etc.)

Pricing science produces 'pricing intelligence' and when implemented well, makes that information available in near real time, to help **Sales Reps price smarter**. It is a capability that keeps the Sales Reps dead center in the decision-making loop and equips them to make better informed pricing decisions.

Another area that I often get asked is how widespread is the use of AI/ML based pricing science. The usual point of the question is to assess the breadth and maturity of the ideas in businesses / industries. I've updated the table in Chapter 9 'The Leadership Challenge', to reflect all the industries I'm personally aware of. I'm sure that it's not an exhaustive list.

Many business leaders wrinkle their foreheads trying to connect classic B-school ideas and the equivalent capabilities in a pricing science approach. Here's a framework I've seen customers use to connect these dots:

- What is my threat of substitutes?
  - o How do customers view my product quality/value vs. their needs and how do they view my competitors' product fit/quality/value?
- What is my market fragmentation assessment?

- o How many real competitors do I have and what is my market position? Am I the 600 lb gorilla or 60 lb chimp, or one in an army of ants…. Can I move the market in some segments?
- What is my capacity/utilization/capital plans situation? At present vs. in next 12-18 months.
- What is my macroeconomic outlook?
- What is my relative price position vs. key competitors?
  - o What are the qualitative advantages of my products vs. competitors? Where am I better? Where are they better?
- What is my short-term plan vs. longer term plan?
  - o Is my intent to emphasize my strengths, or to emphasize competitor's weaknesses? Will I fix my weaknesses, or will I downplay my weaknesses?
- What if a competitor has capacity/production challenges? Do I want to respond?
  - o Does a competitor have recent production/quality or delivery/service issues?
- What is my Go-To-Market plan for a group of products? Is it market share growth, margin rate improvement, maintaining the status quo, or something else?
- What are my goals for specific targeted accounts?
  - o Address shrinking accounts?
  - o Grow existing accounts?
  - o Plans for strategic, growth, or other special accounts?
  - o Goals for new account acquisition?
- What are my goals for specific targeted products?
  - o Have I identified specific products?
  - o Am I introducing new products/lines?
  - o What's my plan/intent regarding underperforming lines?
    - ▪ Make certain products more profitable?
    - ▪ Reallocate production or warehouse capacity better?
- What is my business assessment of the Sales team's <u>designed capability</u> to execute that plan?
  - o Potential factors to consider: territory coverage/# reps, the capability of their inside sales/support. How robust are your sales operations processes?
- What is my business assessment of the Sales team's <u>performance capability</u> to execute that plan?
  - o Potential factors to consider are: How to drive behavior? What training and incentives modifications would improve performance?

What is the specific expertise/capability of the sales team? What are its gaps?

So, <u>assume your business has adopted this 'thought framework'</u> for strategic pricing decisions. What can you do with the results? First, note that a large fraction of the above address price sensitivity concerns and gauging what the market response will be. The other part is focused on organizational capability and readiness. Putting in place an advanced solution that is in sync with business assessments of the market likely response gives you additional 'levers to pull'— these levers connect strategy to executable tactics. The benefits that flow directly are an ability to:

- Challenge long-held assumptions to drive discussion and ownership of prioritized change initiatives.
- Define forward looking intent inputs to drive process change, while also leveraging the derived historical execution insights (aka pricing intelligence) from pricing science techniques.
- Prioritize in a clear-eyed, data-driven way what makes sense vs. what does not.
- Be sober-minded about the people-side of the plan development. Involve stakeholders in the assessment and design, <u>and</u> sell, sell, sell to them — sellers, sales managers, product managers, marketing managers, procurement managers, and finance managers.
- <u>Iteratively</u> refine execution adjustments on a schedule that the business needs, maybe monthly or quarterly, or perhaps a high/low/shoulder season approach.

In summary, **connecting strategy to executable pricing tactics** is very doable. We'll talk more about the techniques, but here are three simple examples:

- Define market intent (market share vs. margin improvement goals) by product line and/or channel and/or customer type and/or order size, etc.
- Define guardrails like minimum margin inputs differently by product, by geography, by customer type, order type, order size, etc.
- Define market-facing inputs to keep prices aligned across customer type, channel, industry, and product. Examples might include the alignment of prices due to reasons related to PLC (product life cycle) or GBB (good, better, best), or geographical reasons.

<u>It's **imperative** that your business establish **an executive level team**, a Pricing Council</u>, that **sets policy and vision** on how the company wants to

synchronize the execution of procurement, manufacturing, marketing, product management, sales, and finance to support the top and bottom-line business objectives, including synchronizing how you set <u>and</u> execute price in the market.

Lastly, business leaders need ways to stay abreast of rapidly changing pricing capabilities and trends, and as starting points I would suggest the following:

- <u>Publications and Groups:</u> Harvard Business Review, Professional Pricing Society Bulletin, Pricing Brew's B2B Pricing Insights and Journal, Journal of Revenue and Pricing Management, Distribution Pricing Journal, INFORMS Journals (there are 17 of them, but I'd suggest the Applied Analytics and the Data Science journals), Silicon Valley Professionals
- <u>Conferences:</u> Professional Pricing Society Conference (US and Europe), European Pricing Platform Conference, Zilliant's Mindshare Conferences (US and Europe), Pricing Strategy USA Summits, Copperberg Manufacturing Pricing Excellence Conference
- <u>Other:</u> MIT Sloan AI/ML courses, and books like those listed in Appendix 1, see both the lists for Pricing References and Non-Pricing References.

Jim Vaughn, Global Head of Pricing Consulting Advisory at Zilliant

Introduction

If you're a NASCAR driver, you can't afford to be leaking fuel on the track. You won't be able to get the power you need. You won't be able to drive as far. You'll have to keep pulling over for more gas while your competitors accelerate around the track.
Ali Velshi, formerly
CNN's Chief Business Correspondent[1]

The Pricing Blindfold

Company profitability revolves around this same basic premise—your business can't get where you want it to go if it is leaking profit. Cost cutting and efficiency gains are harder and harder to come by. That's because of more than thirty years of successful analytical work and process re-engineering aimed at streamlining the supply side of business. And still, we find almost every business under some stress financially. In our globally competitive market, global economic boom or bust, we have increasing price volatility. Raw materials costs and market changes can wreak havoc with your pricing.

In a down market, limiting your price decreases can be very risky, and it is difficult to prevent over discounting in the race to the bottom of the market. When faced with what appear to be the only two options:

    1) losing clients and revenue, or
    2) just losing some revenue,

businesses most often choose the latter. For this reason alone, the one-size-fits-all or across-the-board price decrease is incredibly destructive. One-size-fits-all price decreases can also lead to or accelerate price wars, and I'll guarantee you

1

100% market acceptance. I'll talk about this more later, but clearly if some of your customers are not asking for a price decrease, then unilaterally lowering your price to all customers is not a profit enhancement technique. Similarly, if you are trying to grow market share by lowering your prices, this one-size-fits-all approach will **leak fuel on the track** because you are treating all customers the same, and some channels will not respond with future greater demand.

Conversely, in a rising economy, raising prices via a one-size-fits-all process is an extremely hard sell with your customers (and with your own Sales team). As proof of the challenge, we regularly see that announced price increases of 5% yield only 1-3% or about 1/3 to 2/3 of the increase. I call this the price increase "stickiness factor."

Why is this true? Because the whole underlying premise of announced price increases is wrong-headed. Across-the-board price increases—whether they are for a whole company's products or a product family—aim to raise the average selling price by treating all customers the same. But your customers are not all the same! You probably don't have an 'average customer.' The problem here is that you end up trying to raise prices on customers paying more than the average by the same percentage as customers paying less than the average. You essentially can 'punish' your above average paying customers and your relationship with them via this approach. As an example, *let's say you plan to raise prices by 5%, then for these two customers you will do this:*

Customer	Unit price	Quantity Per Month	Percent Price Change	Dollar Price Change
A	$10/widget	100 widgets	5% price increase	50 cents
B	$8/widget	200 widgets	5% price increase	40 cents

So, for this 1st scenario, this is the best case that could play out: a $130 profit increase per month.

Customer	Dollar Price Change	Quantity Per Month	Profit Increase	
A	50 cents	100 widgets	$50	**Total Profit $130**
B	40 cents	200 widgets	$80	

But Customer A complains to their Sales Rep, so you roll back part of the price increase to Customer A, to say a 3% increase (or 30 cents), and you achieve a total $110 profit increase per month.

Customer	Dollar Price Change	Quantity Per Month	Profit Increase	
				Total Profit $110
A	30 cents	100 widgets	$30	
B	40 cents	200 widgets	$80	

But let's consider a second scenario.

If you knew in advance that Customer A is rather price sensitive and B is not, and you could choose a 3% increase that would be acceptable to Customer A and a 7% increase (or 56 cents) that would be acceptable to Customer B, then we get this.

Customer	Dollar Price Change	Quantity Per Month	Profit Increase	
				Total Profit $142
A	30 cents	100 widgets	$30	
B	56 cents	200 widgets	$112	

Which sounds like a better profit improvement approach to you? An additional $110 or $142 in profits a month?

I'm no expert at mind reading, but I suspect I know your answer. Admitting that your customers are not equal in many ways, including their price sensitivity, can lead to better attempts to group them into categories that are derived from specific buying patterns. Omitting price sensitivity from your customer and product market segmentation creates, at best, a poor proxy for grouping and **limits your ability to minimize profit leakage**.

This commonplace lack of insight into demonstrated price sensitivity and buying patterns when determining B2B (business to business) pricing is akin to a race car driver **racing in a blindfold**. You are racing from pricing event to pricing event without being able to see a good map of the twists, turns, potholes, and pileups in your way. With thousands or tens of thousands of products and thousands of customers with perhaps multiple agreements each, it's easy to see that there are hundreds of thousands of pricing decisions being made, and this lack of insight into a customer's price sensitivity leads to a revenue-focused versus a profit-focused selling process. Not every customer will be as profitable as the next, so determining how to avoid leaving money on the table in any negotiation is a very tricky business. But it is very do-able—I know, I've been doing it for over 30 years. My B2B pricing experience for high and low-tech manufacturers and distributors of commodity to cutting-edge products, coupled with my B2C (business to consumer) pricing experience for telecoms, travel, hospitality, and apartment rentals, has helped me to see a larger series of pricing patterns.

Manufacturers and distributors typically service customers in both the spot market and via longer term agreements. Often, there are only vague assurances regarding volume under a B2B agreement. And because these agreements may have long periods of validity, getting the offered price right is critically important.

The goal of this book is to provide you with:

- Practical insights gleaned from years of pricing experience.
- A roadmap for your business to reap the demonstrated benefits that come from "a pricing science approach."

so that you **stop leaking fuel on the track!**

So, what is "a pricing science approach"? At a very top level, a pricing science approach is more than just math and analytics, it is a proactive pricing approach that is firmly established in data science <u>and</u> business experience.

Peeking Through the Blindfold

Before we jump into the details of pricing, let's add another dimension to our racing imagery, and consider the weather. Clearly, weather conditions are a vital component in Formula One racing, as depicted in the movie *Rush*[2] about Niki Lauda's racing rivalry and near fatal, weather-driven crash during the 1976 German Grand Prix at Nürburgring. Our ability to predict weather conditions accurately and quickly is constantly evolving.

In Niki Lauda's era, we had a few weather satellites, many local weather stations, many commercial aircraft, and we regularly flew planes into hurricanes to get data. The result? We gathered data from many sources and built rudimentary computer-based weather models, but it still was not easy to pull all that data together. Our systems weren't well connected, and our computers weren't very powerful. As a result, we still relied heavily on the expertise and experience of the regional and local weather forecasters. Their job was to make sense of all the conflicting information and to create forecasts that were still in large part anecdotal and were still broad swath forecasts. There were no hourly forecasts, just daily ones.

Now let's consider our current capabilities. Some like to joke about how The Weather Channel™ and the major networks have turned weather into major news events, even before anything happens. Weather forecasts are generally quite accurate because of several new capabilities. We now have large numbers of weather satellites and lots of places all over the world gather ground temperatures, ocean temperatures, winds, humidity, pressure, and cloud cover data. We gather weather data not just 24 hours a day; we gather it at least 1440 minutes a day, and we hold on to all that data. In parallel with improving our data acquisition, we have been creating more powerful computers and bigger networks that allow us to get that data. And using the data in an automated way, we now have very sophisticated forecast models that help us improve decision making—should I take an umbrella, or should I evacuate ahead of the coming hurricane?

An interesting point on the growth of computing capabilities came from Paul Otellini, CEO of Intel, at the 2010 Consumer Electronic Show. He compared the progress of computing to automotive advancements, saying that if the automotive industry had kept pace proportionally with improvements of the computer processor industry, then cars would go 470,000 miles per hour, get 100,000 miles per gallon and cost 3 cents.[3]

Because of this convergence of big data, computing power, and machine learning, we can very accurately forecast the weather hourly. However, we still want a meteorologist to look at the results from the many weather forecasts and decide how to best use them. So, what is going on here? We:

- gather data,
- turn data into information,
- turn information into actionable intelligence,
- advise people proactively and accurately what to expect,
- so that people can make decisions.

In the last 40 years, the same quiet improvements of weather forecasting have been happening in business too. We see everywhere that companies have put in place large data warehouses, Enterprise Resource Planning (ERP) systems, and quoting tools. These systems store all sorts of transactional data about the business environment (as opposed to the physical environment data for weather). Meanwhile, we have also made significant advances in pricing by creating very sophisticated pricing models. We can tease out of transactional data things like complex demand patterns; customer and product context-sensitive price pressures; and other important attributes that help us understand the market. This major leap forward, although quiet, means that it's now possible for pricing to do what we take for granted when we think about the weather.

**You can do a lot more than just peek
through the blindfold!**

A Quick Book Overview

Many of you will enjoy reading this book from front to back just the way I wrote it, but others of you will want to find the areas that interest you the most and skip around. To help you understand the flow, I've laid out the major topics in each chapter for you.

Chapters 1 & 2: These two introductory chapters highlight the fundamental ideas of pricing and talk to a variety of cross-industry pricing pain points, including:

- Why businesses need to price differently?
- Why a one-size-fits-all price change hurts profitability?
- How traditional market segmentation and analytical techniques attempt to improve profitability.
- Why the existing approaches leave a lot of money on the table?

Chapter 3: Addresses the traditional approaches to price setting, covering:

- Why a purely analytics-based approach is not scalable in most businesses?
- Why pricing analytics, like price waterfalls, are useful but are not a silver bullet?

Chapter 4: Further develops many of the ideas in the prior chapters and provides the larger context of the pricing problem, including:

- Further discussion on the scalability problems of a purely business intelligence-driven pricing solution.
- A broad discussion of price segmentation and its benefits.

Chapter 5: Describes at a high-level the major pieces of a pricing science-based solution:

- An overview of the four main steps in pricing science design.
- How a pricing science approach gives Sales more confidence to negotiate in a market-aware price range.

Chapter 6: Addresses why pricing science solutions allow Sales to be more effective:

- How pricing science improves Sales negotiating effectiveness.
- How pricing science helps Sales avoid pricing too low or too high.

Chapter 7: This chapter includes several short sections on some of the more complex pricing challenges, including:

- Market price variation
- Composite/made-to-order products
- Freight

- Rebates
- Assessing the impact of new prices.

Chapter 8: Highlights the successes from two quite different clients:

- The Shaw Industries story.
- The United Rentals story.

Chapter 9: My concluding chapter talks to executive leadership and its critical roles in visibly committing to a pricing science approach to improve profitability, specifically:

- Improving profitability is not just a technical task, it is a leadership and management challenge.
- Why leaders must demonstrate commitment to any pricing improvement initiative.
- The clear need for an executive Pricing Council.

Chapter 1
Fundamental Ideas

The market is tough, competitors are entering and leaving your markets at an accelerating pace. Prices are changing rapidly. Product lifecycles seem to get shorter and shorter. Globalization makes cost fluctuations a constant challenge. Managing these constantly fluctuating facets requires an ongoing, dynamic review and reassessment of discounts for new and existing customer opportunities. Because of all of this, pricing is hard to get "right."

Pricing certainly involves many people in multiple roles in most companies. These companies have invested lots of time and energy in tools to execute a pricing strategy. Typical examples include ERP pricing modules, business intelligence tools, data warehouses, and various legacy quoting systems or extraordinarily complex spreadsheets.

These systems have layers upon layers, which makes them hard to manage or even understand. But these systems have varying degrees of one core idea in mind—namely, *not all customers are willing to pay the same price* for a particular widget. Otherwise, you would only need one price point per product.

The reasons for offering different customers different pricing seem to be over 90% the same in every industry I've worked with:

- Bigger customers expect to pay less and bargain for that advantage.
- Different competitors in different geographies make some markets more price competitive.
- Different competitors in different channels make some channels more price competitive.
- Some customer industries are more or less price sensitive than others.
- Some customers buy a wider mix of products from you.

- Sales believes they can "grow" a customer relationship and their value to your company.
- And the list can go on and on.

The core of all this is the recognition that all customers do not value your product equally and you don't value all your customers equally. A core component of this is the classic price-quantity demand tradeoff: you will probably sell more of something at lower price points and fewer of something when you raise your price. You can't control how much a customer values your product, but you have a choice on which price points you offer to which customers.

Some customers may see a price decrease while others see an increase. One of the core objectives of pricing science is to match pricing more closely to the value the customer perceives. This creates a "win-win" situation.

In Chart 1, if the "true price" the customer is willing to pay is $120 (see Willingness to Pay in the glossary) then offering a price less than that leaves money on the table (lost profits), and conversely if your price is too high you will not get the sale (and lose both revenue and profit)—both of these pricing scenarios **spill fuel on the track!**

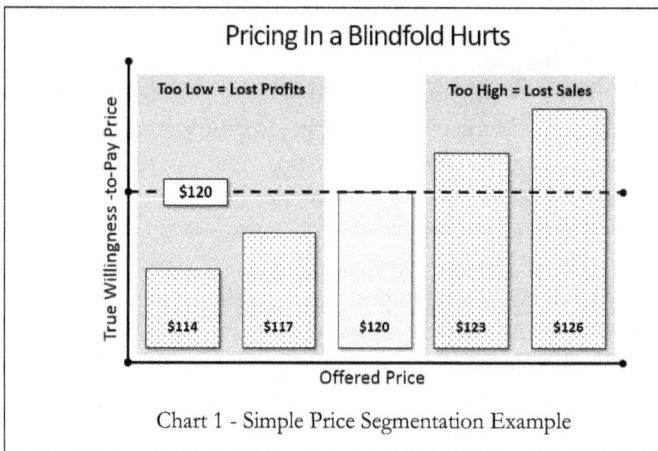

Chart 1 - Simple Price Segmentation Example

A quick Google search will reveal many references to material[4] focused on what can be learned through:

- Price waterfalls and differing costs-to-serve.
- The importance of setting initial product prices for customers.
- Creating hurdles or channels.
- Considering the total customer value.
- Understanding how much a customer values your product is unrelated to your costs.

Many authors have also addressed the importance of segmenting your customers, understanding the value those customers place on your products, and using that to drive price setting.[5] This approach has great merit and is certainly supportive in new product launches or re-launches (including lifecycle adjustments). Properly positioning the product in the market is important to buying market share, accreting margin, or recouping as quickly as possible some of the R&D dollars and effort to bring the product to market.

What almost every author glosses over is a method to set and control pricing in a mid to high-volume environment in the lengthy middle of the product lifecycle—whether that involves agreements or price lists or spot transactions. What we see instead is a lot of Sales and Marketing price actions in which someone says, "Let's launch this trial price change in a small part of the market and we can track how our customers respond." The problem is that even if it is well executed, it is still just anecdotal—you can't be confident that you can extrapolate from this small "test balloon" to the rest of your business.

Pricing Intelligence?

The challenge most of us face is a lack of actionable pricing intelligence (not just where is the market, but in what range should we price this opportunity) and a mechanism to coherently manage day-to-day volume in a proactive manner in a hyperactive market.

Unless you are lucky enough to have a large and very experienced staff of pricing analysts and very few pricing decisions to make across your whole company, this "test balloon" highly manual pricing approach is impractical. In companies with large numbers of agreements or large numbers of quote opportunities a day, a manual analytics approach is simply not scalable.

Most likely, some of you also are aware of a few voices that will claim that while segmenting your customers on "willingness to pay" is theoretically possible, it is just not practical to create an accurate price elasticity (or price sensitivity) measure. On this last topic, frequently the objections are along the line of a Professional Pricing Society blog from 2012, where this opinion generated many comments:

> "...I don't believe transactional data will lead to an accurate or reliable measure of price elasticity. There are many drivers beyond transactional data that have an impact on price sensitivity. For example, drivers such as a constantly changing competitive and technology landscape,

sales force effectiveness, fluctuations in product mix, and global pricing methods, and many more…" [6]

By analogy, this point of view is akin to saying a NASCAR or Formula 1 or Moto Grand Prix team can't predict exactly how the weather will affect a particular race—they can't predict exactly how much fuel their driver needs because there are too many weather variables. Varying air temperature and humidity affect fuel combustion; temperature changes create changes in drag and the wear rate of the tires, which alters traction; and there are many more factors. The problem with this perspective is that it implies that any model that is not 100% perfect is not valuable.

Many years ago, a professional mentor, General Dave Maddox, told me when I was starting grad school to remember that the 100% solution three weeks late was of no value, but the 80% solution on time is immensely valuable when it comes to making decisions. (BTW, General Maddox was the lead for all mathematical analytics work in the US Army and later the Commanding General of NATO—in summary, a very smart leader!)

Similarly, George Box, one of the most respected statisticians of the 20th century, wrote in his 1987 book *Empirical Model-Building and Response Surfaces*, "Remember that all models are wrong; the practical question is how wrong do they have to be to not be useful." [7] Are weather models perfect? No. Are they useful? Very much so!

You Can Segment Based on Price Sensitivity

Some will continue to claim price elasticity calculations are not possible or useful, but I will assert that the likely causes of price variation can be assessed in a business context. Vilfredo Pareto is an Italian economist you probably have heard of. My view is aligned with his ideas in 1906, which you know as the Pareto Principal.

It is also called the 80/20 rule, or the idea "the vital few versus the trivial many," and is core to many approaches that aim to create a better understanding of a problem and find a solution. Of the maybe 10-20 variables that might affect price and volume, only a few will have a routine and dominant effect. Understanding how maybe 6 to 12 factors have routinely impacted your transactional pricing over time is key to better understanding price elasticity.

Further, when you combine transactional data with business insights and a good understanding of products and customers, you can calculate incredibly useful values for elasticity at the micro-market segment level. For instance, low-margin, high-volume products are considered by some types of customers to be commodities. Any attempt to raise prices for those product-and-customer cases will impact demand quickly. However, for other customers who buy the same product infrequently, a price increase will have little to no effect on the demand.

Here's a simple example. Raising the price on a carton of paper by 25 cents will get little to no response from a mom-and-pop pizza shop that buys three cartons a month but will generate a big response from the commercial printer that consumes 50 cartons an hour. Combining transactionally determined elasticity information with a good business understanding of the customer, product, and order factors allows you to calculate a viable price sensitivity value.

Divide your market into pricing micro-segments and look at the transactions counts at each and every particular price point. The historical price distributions reflect where you have been successful at winning business—what prices are viable with what customer groups.

What can the various shapes in Chart 2 tell us about viable prices in a micro-segment of the market?[8] We can observe that both micro-segments have about the same "middle of the market" price just below $30.

But we can also see that in the segment on the right there is a truly clear drop-off in historical business above the low $30 range. In the other, prices in the low $40 range have some market traction. Last, we can see that offering a

Price Distributions Reflect Price Sensitivity

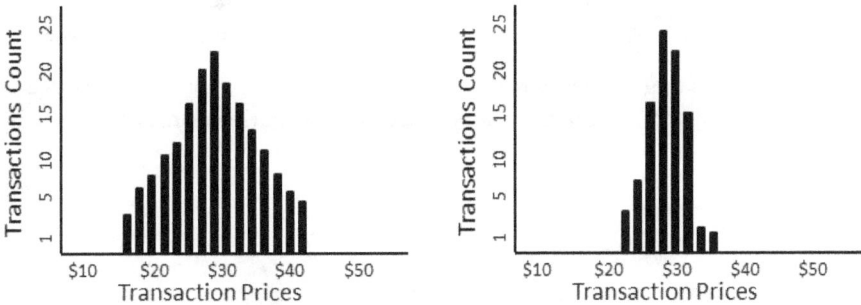

Chart 2 - Price Distribution Shapes

price in the teens does not seem to be warranted in one segment. Let's assume for a minute that the only difference in these two micro-segments is related to geography. Attempting to raise prices above $35 in the graph on the right would bring a greater risk of a drop in demand because the customers in this micro-segment seem only to be willing to buy in a much narrower price range. Knowledge like this is very valuable in order to gain insights into price sensitivity, we should be asking questions like these:

- How are prices distributed in a micro-segment? Do prices look like a typical bell curve, or do they have a long tail to the left or right?
- Do prices under similar circumstances have a wide or narrow range?
- Is there a large fraction of the historical demand at the most frequently occurring price?

> *I have been using the above approach for over 15 years to illustrate how one can interpret transactional distributions and understand price sensitivities, but the actual approach is mathematically a good bit more complex.*

Without jumping too far ahead, a short intro to the ideas that help us calculate price sensitivity will help you grasp the main concepts. You might ask, "How does one create the price distributions in Chart 2?" Micro-market price segmentation involves picking the strongest price predictors using some science-based (AI-ML) techniques (e.g., classification, regression, clustering, and others). The primary goals of price segmentation are to group your transactions into micro-segments and create a way to properly compare "apples-to-apples" buying circumstances. Or, to put it in different terms, accurately identify comparable products sold to similar customers under similar conditions. Or in a bit more "math-y" terminology:

- Minimize the price differences within micro-segments.
- Maximize the price differences between micro-segments.
- Provide a basis to calculate price sensitivity within each micro-segment.

Illustrating this visually might look like Chart 3, where we plot price and quantity and then create clusters based on that transactional data. Based on

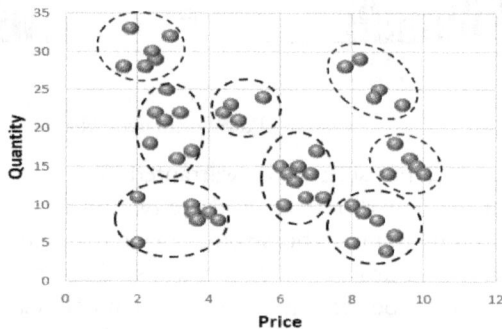

Chart 3 - Price vs. Quantity Clusters

the resulting graph, we might conclude that certain transactions "belong together" based on the above three goals.

We can depict each one of the above groups in Chart 4 with price points along the horizontal axis and the frequency of selling at that price point on the vertical axis.

Distribution of Prices

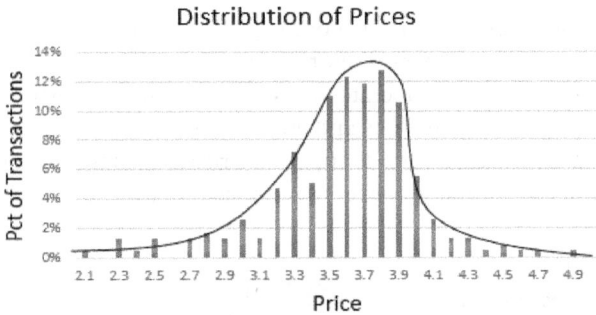

Chart 4 - Price Segment Distribution

In each of these small slices of the market, you then have insight into the distribution of price points which includes the center point of the market as well as some insight into reasonable upper and lower boundaries of where this small market slice has typically transacted business.

Distribution of Prices

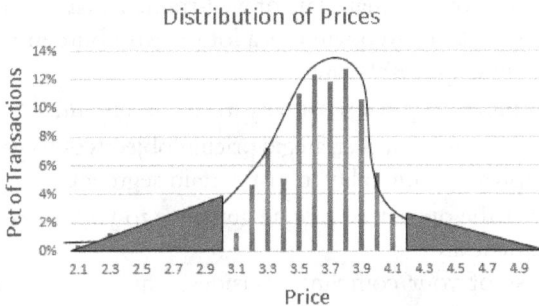

Chart 5 - Price Segment Guidance

Then, from a pure business intelligence reporting perspective, one could give the price negotiator some center point and price range to operate in. But of course, this only tells you what you have done in the past; it does not allow you to change your market-facing revenue versus profit objectives.

Can you imagine the army of analysts you would need, and the number of working hours to produce analysis like this on an ad hoc basis each time a quoting opportunity or price negotiation occurs?

Let's say your company has only 500 products and 500 customers. You view your customers as Small, Medium, and Large, based on sales, and they come from five distinct channels or industries. Your customers can buy from you via a spot-market price and longer-term pre-negotiated agreements.

To support the spot-market quoting, you have used 5 quantity break tiers in the past. Your Sales team operates across the country in what you believe are 5 major markets, 5 minor markets and an "everything else" market. To respond accurately to a potential quote, then, your pricing analysts would have to be intimately familiar with and have data available to chart and assess price distributions for:

- 500 products
- 3 customer sizes
- 2 types of pricing agreements (spot or longer term)
- 5 customer channels
- 5 quantity break tiers
- 11 markets: 5 major markets or 5 minor markets or the "everything else" market.

Multiplying those, it shows there are possibly 825,000 distinct selling circumstances they need to be familiar with, and they would all have to be trained to visually interpret those 825,000 charts and provide pricing insights similarly.

Last, even if you had that army of well-trained analysts, it still would not get that pricing to the Sales Rep without a lot of extra burden on your Sales team. But an algorithmic approach can:

- Determine the price sensitivity in each segment,
- Blend that with new strategic pricing objectives to grow market share or improve profitability in just certain segments,
- Deliver the optimized pricing guidance to your sales reps systematically.

Regardless of your company's business environment, understanding and exercising your pricing levers are the most direct way to improve your profitability. Many authors have written about a 1% increase in price leading to a typical 8% to 11% increase in profit[9]. So, we are not talking about major price changes.

I once worked with a national broad line distributor. By their own analysis, they had concluded that a 1 cent increase in price on every item on every transaction would generate well over $50M dollars of additional pure profit each year. And they were quite confident that a 1 cent price increase on a package of toilet tissue was not going to drive away any customer that they really wanted to be servicing.

As stated before, the primary focus of this book is on the price setting challenges of manufacturers and distributors, and I will talk specifically to four main "pricing vehicles": List pricing, Matrix pricing, Negotiated Long-Term agreement pricing, and Negotiated Spot-Market pricing. My goal is to help you accomplish your job, close the deal, minimize the chance you leave money on the table, and respond to strategic initiatives to improve margins or buy market share in some region or channel or segment—put another way, to help you stop leaking fuel on the track and win the race.

The Seven Keys to Pricing for Profit

This leads me to my Seven Keys to Pricing[10]:

1. **Focus on the Price** Your customers are not equal. Have price levels to allow you to sell your products at profit margins appropriate to each group of customers. Grapple with the question of what business to take at what price. At various times different selling circumstances drive different answers, create a "win-win," and know when to walk away from some business.
2. **Like Politics, all Pricing is Local** Your internal costs don't matter to your customers, they are your problem to manage. Decouple your prices from your costs. American business has a long history of cost-based pricing (rather than value-based pricing).
3. **Know Your Customers' Price Sensitivities** In order to effectively implement market-based pricing you must know the buying behaviors of your customers. Price segmentation must be based on buying behaviors, NOT things like zip codes, average selling prices, average revenue levels, rules of thumb, etc.
4. **Know Your More Valuable Customer Traits** Reward those more valuable customers with your better/best pricing. How you define your most valuable customers may vary.
5. **Data-Informed, Not Gut-Feel Decisions Will Drive New Profits** Gathering data does NOT help, unless you do something with it. Data must be turned into usable information, and turned into actionable intelligence, which is predictively used in the pricing process.

6. **Know and Exploit Each Product's Value Cycle**

   a. For a new product that is generating lots of interest you should be charging different prices to various customer segments based on the perceived value in those segments.

   b. For a product becoming more main stream pricing is more Sales management driven, you may sell it to a wider array of customers at a wider number of price points.

   c. For a product that is becoming a commodity, decide whether to continue to make it and sell at lower margins, sell the rights to another party, or drop it and re-allocate the production capacity or shelf space to a more profitable product.

7. **Market Agility: Constantly Re-evaluate Your Revenue and Margin Trade-offs**

   a. Today's market is very dynamic, predictive pricing intelligence needs to be pushed out to the people making pricing decisions every hour. In many B2B industries, I see a need to recalculate price sensitivities and decide at least weekly when to update pricing guidance in the market. Rarely does negotiated pricing guidance age well at three months old.

   b. For digitized channels, your plans for market-facing pricing must include at least near real-time price adjustments for some (or maybe all) customer demand streams.

   c. Omni-channel price synchronization should not be construed to mean the same price in every channel for every customer all the time. Think about how to orchestrate this to meet strategic business objectives.

Chapter 2
Pan-Industry Pricing Pain Points

A Game of Chicken?

Senior executives, middle managers, product line managers and Sales Reps have to grapple with the question "can we <u>successfully</u> close the deal at this price?" They are mystified by the absence of a good, clearly defined price-setting process for new and existing customers.

These same people often feel lucky to have some accepted rules of thumb or home-grown metrics to guide them, because these rules provide them with some 'top cover' in case things don't pan out well. Sometimes these decision makers lack even that.

The linkage between a company's strategic vision, the value of its products or services to its customers, and the pricing of those products or services is often a chasm that has never been crossed. Sales is typically sent two implicitly conflicting messages: "make your sales quotas (…at all costs)" and "don't give away too much."

As a client's Sales VP said to me, "It often becomes a game of chicken to close the deal because we just don't have good metrics that can guide us in negotiation." This leaves the B2B sales process in a quandary. And to be honest, ultimately whatever drives the greatest sales compensation, not company profitability, usually wins out in the price negotiation process.

Companies often employ a variety of "basic pricing strategies" to go to market, for example:

- Cost-plus or minimum markup strategies
- Maintain margin or margin float strategies

- Match the competitor strategies
- What did they pay last time?
- And the old standby, "use your experience, that's what we are paying you for."

These pricing strategies are usually built on not one but TWO houses of cards, namely the average selling price and the cost. If your company is a manufacturer with multiple plants (maybe in multiple countries with multiple currencies), you know that the attributed cost is mostly an accounting driven exercise and has nothing to do with the market value of a product.

If you are a distributor, you may have a pretty good idea what a product costs because you get invoiced—but what is the best cost to use: the replacement cost, the LIFO or FILO cost, the average warehouse/yard cost, or the post year-end rebate adjusted cost? Really, it's still a mess! And when you add in the fully loaded cost allocation, it looks a lot like the manufacturer's cost allocation problem.

Various industries do a better (or worse) job of maintaining timely cost data. In the last five years, I literally have seen the gamut from more frequent than weekly cost updates, to annual and longer cost updates.

Also, pricing is often in no-man's land organizationally. Sometimes the "head pricer" (if there is one) reports to the CFO, or the VP of Sales, or the VP of Marketing. Sometimes pricing is decentralized, and resources are scattered in regional headquarters in order to make it more in tune with field Sales. Frequently the "head pricer" (or group of people) reports according to some byzantine organizational rules that are not particularly in sync with the company's strategic vision that leverages the value of its products to its customers.

Regardless of the above, whether a company chooses a centralized or decentralized pricing organization, and regardless of which power center the pricing function reports to, your company can reap vast benefits from improving the way prices are set.

The last pain point is miscommunication. People often use terms loosely and in conflicting ways even between divisions of the same company. For example, net price vs. gross price: Is net price the pocket price or the grossed up invoiced price or something else?

Similarly, some industries use the term Customer Specific Agreement (CSA) to refer to a distributor's Into Stock pricing agreement, while others will use CSA to mean a distributor's "rebate" agreement to service particular end customers.

While working with a large electrical manufacturer to implement a data-informed, science-based approach to pricing, I spent the better part of three months just getting the four primary business units to agree on standard terminology. I worked with them to resolve topics as simple as the meaning of "customer specific agreement" and what was the default length of such an agreement. This allowed me to talk to the "pricers" in each business unit to gather requirements and prevent miscommunication.

Terms of Reference in This Book

For the sake of clarity in this book, I'm setting out some common terms of reference. So, if your industry uses a term to mean something different you should be able to map my book terms to your definitions.

There are several B2B **pricing vehicles,** but generally they can be described by the following:

- "The" List Price
- Matrix Pricing (for Customer Tiers/Buckets/Groups Assignment)
- Promotional Pricing
- Override Pricing
- New Product Pricing
- Negotiated Pricing
    - o   Customer Agreements
    - o   Spot/Project Quotes

Let's define these terms in an abbreviated way. A more detailed definition of terms can be found in the Glossary.

- "The" List Price is mostly a positioning statement in the market. Sometimes it can also be a catalog or web price. Typically, it is set by a central authority and updated infrequently per product. List Price sales are a special B2B pricing situation in which there is little to nothing known about the customer, and there is no price negotiation.
- The Matrix Price approach is typically derived from and associated with marketing programs employing tiers / buckets /groups associated with price levels. In the Matrix Price problem, we know who the customer is and what products they are eligible to buy from a Matrix Price list. The Matrix Price is usually calculated via a multiplier applied to a reference price such the List Price and has many common names such as Column Price, Price Tier, Level, Price List or even List Price.
- Promotional Pricing is typically attributed to be for some short-term purpose such as "buying market share in Los Angeles for product family

Y." Often Promotional Pricing is "owned" by a central authority, such as Marketing, and supports a specific market communication plan.

- Price Overrides often come from highly decentralized decision making, varying from one pricing decision to the next. They serve for four main purposes: 1) to correct for a perceived mistake in the price list that someone else has carefully set, 2) to correct for some other administrative error, 3) to mitigate a customer relationship issue or 4) to try to "juice" demand through a onetime special offer. It is often misused for end-of-the-quarter specials, which simply pull forward later demand and **leak fuel on the track**.

- New Product Pricing is performed by Product Managers for market positioning and may attempt to reclaim R&D investments early in a product's lifecycle.

- Negotiated B2B **pricing vehicles** include:
  - o Customer Specific Agreements (CSA) - Manufacturers that sell via distributors utilize "into stock" agreements to control product and price availability. Distributors hold stock for resale.
  - o "Blanket pricing" Agreements (BA) - Manufacturers sometimes sell directly to other OEM-type customers. These other manufacturers do not hold stock for re-sale. Manufacturers may also establish Blanket Agreements with "Agents" who do not hold stock for resale. These agents essentially serve as non-company commissioned sales brokers.
  - o Special Price Agreements (SPA) or rebates - Manufacturers may establish rebate agreements with distributors to service a special customer. The special customer's re-sale price may be near or below the distributor's "into stock" price. So, the manufacturer pays a rebate to the Distributor to provide the service and "make them whole."
  - o Casual or Spot-Market or Project Quotes (SQ) - OEM-type customers, distributors or agents can request more aggressive pricing for opportunities when firm quantities are usually well known.

Chapter 3
Traditional Approaches to Price Setting

Business intelligence tools are great, but they are not our salvation in the 'pricing space'

"He's reacting to a shift in the market that only he can hear."

Reactive (Not Predictive)

As many have written, we should compare the prices paid for a product with customers in the same group. But unless those customers are aligned into groups based on soundly identified drivers of price, your comparison is not likely to be actionable.

For instance, if you compare two customers in the same region who are both buying from the same family of products, you might conclude that one is getting "brother-in-law prices," and one is happily paying slightly more than the market seems to usually bear. And as a result, you'd be tempted to tell Sales Management to push the "brother-in-law pricing" up 5-7% the next time.

Let's say you have really drilled down and find these customers are in the same geographical group, are similar in size ($250K-500K annual sales) and are both independent widget distributors. You would argue that the customers are comparable. But what if I then said one only buys from your 'economy line' products, and the other buys higher margin products in that product family and also buys from four of your five major product families?

Essentially, one customer is a low-margin, low-touch customer, and the other is a strong business partner but requires specialized billing and has much higher costs-to-serve. Now what does that do to your assessment of price relative to other customers in the same grouping? Clearly tools like price waterfalls that reveal the pocket price and other analytics employing special key performance indicators (KPIs) and related profitability metrics might reveal a hugely different answer to the question 'is this customer priced right?'

Pricing analytics is a crucial tool to manage and can help steer your company to higher profits over a longer period. But pricing analytics is a necessary but not sufficient condition to maximize your profitability—because you are still effectively **racing in a blindfold.**

Attempting to set and execute pricing in an operational setting using only "rear-view mirror" metrics is, by definition, not proactive. And it is not a scalable solution for businesses with moderate quoting volumes. "Rear-view mirror" analytics **leave fuel on the track** that someone must re-actively address the next time you can adjust pricing, in the meantime you will be leaking profits.

So how we can use those pricing analytics tools to help us gain some insight, especially during the initial product rollout or re-launch, or in the assignment of customers into typical marketing programs employing tiers (or buckets or groups) associated with price levels.

Many companies roll out new products via a well-structured and exhaustive process on a lengthy timeline. Many stakeholders may be involved to position the product well in the market. Typically, this positioning revolves around the pricing context and assessment of customer value. Micro-market price segmentation can inform this positioning effort to support fine-tuning price relative to reference products.

But even more importantly, what happens after the first 3-6 months of sales? While stand-alone pricing analytics is not the silver bullet to **stop spilling fuel on the track,** when coupled with a pricing science approach it can provide a crucial link to understanding where profits are being lost and communicating progress to the rest of the organization in simple and understandable terms.

The Price Waterfall

One core element of price analytics is the price waterfall. The overall structure of the price waterfall is important as it provides a truly clear way to understand where your company is leaking profit. All P&L owners, Sales Reps, pricing analysts and product managers should understand it. As shown in Chart 6, across the price waterfall from left to right, there should be positive revenue bars for List Price, Invoice Price and Net Price or Pocket Price. Additionally, there will be several intermediate cost bars that indicate how the revenue bar on the left was decremented to get to the revenue bar on the right.[11] The chart depicts the most typical elements of revenue and cost that should be represented. The general intent is simply to **see where a company is leaking fuel on the track** and thus improve its profitability by addressing these profit leaks.

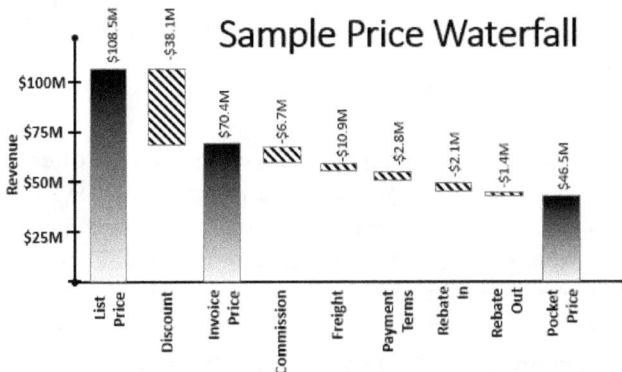

Chart 6 - Sample Price Waterfall

List price—This is the logical place that every price waterfall should start, using a List or max achievable price. As a recent client said to me, we don't really have a defined List Price that <u>our customers are aware of</u>. But internally, to make the pricing process more structured and transparent, this is a good place to start. This waterfall is, after all, an internal tool.

Invoice price—Many companies define the invoice price as some reference or List price minus any <u>on</u>-invoice discounts (discounts explicitly shown on the invoice). Note that invoice price, if defined this way, does not reflect the true value or profitability of a transaction since it does not account for any <u>off</u>-invoice discounts and/or customer-specific costs (cost-to-serve differences). Even so, the invoice price should be an element of the price waterfall, since this is what Sales usually discusses. Only when Sales can view the invoice price on the waterfall, will they get the rationale of the price waterfall chart.

Net price and Pocket price—Simply put, Net Price is Invoice Price minus the effects of all <u>off</u>-invoice discounts. To get from Invoice Price to Net Price on the waterfall there should be a separate bar for each cost-to-serve element you track, e.g., rebates, terms & conditions, and other costs. Some companies show Net and Pocket separately, others simply show the additional cost elements to get to Pocket Price and skip the Net Price column. Pocket Price reflects what the company is actually earning in a transaction. Pocket Price equals the Net Price minus all attributed costs, which may include:

- Transaction costs: internal and external freight, expedited order costs, cost of non-standard/special orders, etc.
- Service costs: Sales team commissions/bonuses, customer service overhead, training, promotions, cost of credit, etc.

Driving Without a Map

After a new product launch many B2B executives are often disappointed in a product's performance from a lifecycle point of view.[12] In the rear-view mirror, more often than not, the actual results (the Pocket Price) bear little resemblance to the pricing assumptions and profitability projections used in the market positioning analysis which in part were used to justify the development and production.

At the beginning of the car race (the product lifecycle), all the indications are that your new car is well-positioned, but during the middle laps, the price levels and profit-performance start to drift in the curves.

Many manufacturers will attribute this drift dynamic to unforeseeable factors. These factors may include competitive entries into the market or macroeconomic demand fluctuations. Of course, this view is completely valid, and these factors will always play a role in price setting and profitability during a product's lifecycle.

This is an example of the "all forecasts are wrong" problem. But there is another factor, some observers would assume that the product management will be actively adjusting the pricing throughout every stage of a product's lifecycle. But the reality is not at all like that.

Product management is usually focused on managing the introduction of new products—launching the latest-and-greatest version of products into the

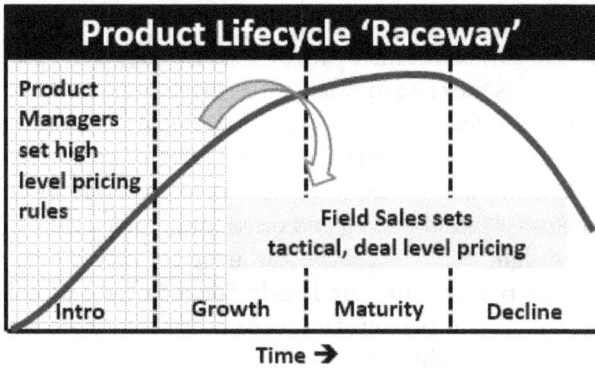

Chart 7 - Product Lifecycle Racetrack

fast lane on the track. Given that this is their prime focus, it's not surprising product management gives less and less time to more mature products.

In the new product launch process, product managers and marketing managers do all sorts of complex, value-based pricing research. This analysis probably includes multiple price points for channel, for geography, and for other facets of the market. This involves analysis to estimate volumes, revenues, and profits over the initial parts of the lifecycle.

Product managers may even spend time working with early customers to get the initial production volumes flowing. And they also may be involved in training the Sales staff on the new features and benefits.

However, once a new product has completed the first few laps of the race using the product manager's pricing guidelines, it is normal for product managers to then shift their focus to the next new product on the roadmap. An implicit passing of control of pricing occurs, from strategic launch pricing to tactical Sales pricing. Unkindly, the product is "thrown over the fence" after a successful introduction. The problem is that it's common for a product to spend 75 percent (or more) of its lifecycle under the day-to-day management of a Sales team (see Chart 7 above).

I once had a circuit protection industry client tell me that their products have lifecycles over 40 years! In their case, a product might easily spend more than 95% of its lifecycle outside of the direct purview of product management's more rigorous analysis and assessment process.

Very often the tactical pricing capabilities in Sales lack a high degree of formality and precision and more often pricing and discounting decisions are made based on "gut feel" or some simple rules of thumb in a "game of chicken." A recent customer's own analysis showed that before their implementation of the new science-based pricing guidance, over 50% of the prices approved by Sales were in contravention of existing policies such as an absolute minimum price.

This statement is not meant to throw Sales under the bus! In fact, the minimum price policies they had in place weren't well fitted to the actual market niches price levels. So, the Sales team fell back on the last-price-paid by the customer or into the groove of offering the same price to everyone regardless of circumstances. And in many cases, the incentive compensation plans in Sales actually worked against sound pricing and discounting practices.

What's the insight here? Typically, the majority of a product's lifecycle occurs under pricing practices that are largely uncontrolled and uninformed by accurate and detailed micro-market data. Because of this, it's quite predictable that overall lifecycle profitability won't be in line with a product manager's initial market expectations or projections.

What can you do? One course of action would be to create an army of analysts to inspect every opportunity's pricing. But supply chain quality managers already know that the 100% inspection approach is not a sound, cost effective method to find defects. Inspecting every price should not be expected to get you where you want to be—but some companies still try!

By funneling deals back through product management or this army of pricing analysts for approval, the expectation is that deal-level pricing decisions will have a greater degree of consistency, accuracy, and profitability.

Not surprisingly, these companies find that all these extra people aren't much better at tactical pricing than Sales. This army of pricing analysts becomes overwhelmed by the ad hoc nature and volume of pricing decisions that need to be made. They can only apply business-driven rules in a specific order, which may not be best for each selling circumstance they encounter.

Also, people just don't quickly pick up on small, incremental changes in the market. It's been repeatedly shown that people are late in responding to market changes until they are significantly obvious.

Another course of action to address the issue is via strict enforcement of pricing rules and policies. Rather than hiring an army of analysts, product managers are told to establish acceptable, static price levels throughout the entire lifecycle, and Sales Reps are expected to adhere strictly to those prices. Of course, this again does not address the core problem.

The product managers lack the time and insights to create and maintain rules and policies that cover the entire lifecycle of all the products. They cannot possibly create rules manually that reflect the wide range of deal-circumstances and price-sensitivities. Last, because products and markets change at different rates over time, any such rules won't stay current. When companies go down this path, they can't help but **spill fuel on the track**.

The only practical alternative is a different course of action to close the tactical pricing gap. Instead of the prior approaches, businesses are putting 'science-y' techniques to use and are creating very granular and specific pricing that stays in tune with their markets without manual intervention.

By using pricing software to automatically distill the newest market-driven pricing intelligence from the latest sales, a company can share it with other Sales Reps when the next price setting event is taking place. This pricing intelligence and price optimization approach applies innovative statistical and mathematical models to the mountains of big data being generated by Sales Reps.

A forward-looking company can determine their customers' price sensitivities on a deal-by-deal, line-item-by-line-item basis. This provides market agility and great accuracy, in a scalable way. These companies can provide actionable pricing guidance – the right price at the right time to the right customer—**where the rubber meets the track**—through relatively simple integrations with their existing quoting and sales tools. These companies get accurate and precise pricing intelligence to their Sales Reps without additional work on the part of Sales Rep.

Traditional B2B Pricing Vehicles

We are at the bread-and-butter level of B2B pricing: List Pricing, Matrix Pricing, and Negotiated Pricing. In many industries, the heavy lifting occurs in one or more varieties of these. The picture in Chart below may help you visualize how the various **pricing vehicles** are related. Also, Chart 36 in Appendix 2: Glossary of Terms, will provide more details.

Business pricing spans a full range of pricing vehicles from "The" List (or even higher than List in some rare cases) to price points lower than any Matrix pricing. Typically, "The" List Price has some very generic Terms & Conditions associated with it. The Matrix (or multiple price points) approach will contain some additional Terms and Conditions but also brings with it some additional advantages. For example, manufacturers and distributors may offer tiers or membership programs which entitle their customers to buy products at the appropriately discounted price points and receive additional benefits like free or

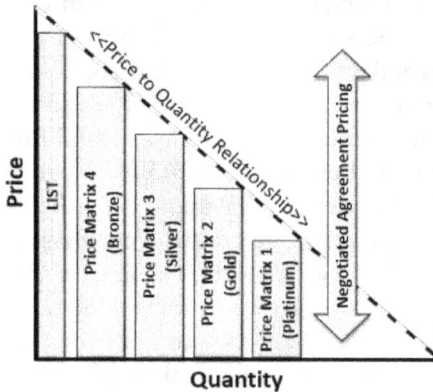

Chart 8 - Price-Quantity Relationship & Price Methods

discounted technical product training for technical Sales staff. In my simple example in Chart 8, there are four tiers or Matrix price levels that could be based on annual spend, or geography, or industry affiliation, or some combination of customer factors—let's call these levels Bronze, Silver, Gold and Platinum.

Although Chart 8 could be read to imply that there is some firm price to quantity relationship in Matrix pricing, that is rather tenuous.

Typically, Matrix prices (multiple price points associated with customer tiers or levels) are offered because a company believes there is sufficient additional market share to make offering a lower price viable for your business. On the other hand, there is a much stronger price versus quantity relationship for negotiated pricing (CSA, SPA, BA, and SQ), denoted by the arrow on the right of the chart. These negotiated pricing vehicles bring with them higher administrative burdens associated with managing varying start and end dates, varying durations, multiple price levels, and specific Terms and Conditions.

Negotiated pricing becomes much more daunting when coupled with possibly thousands of customers and tens of thousands of products in a high quoting/transaction environment. How do you create and manage a "tickler file" to make sure none of these pricing vehicles gets sideways? Simply put, it's a massive challenge to manage and as a result a price matrix approach may be appealing.

In short, there are some tradeoffs between the Matrix price (or multiple price point) approach and the Negotiated price approach. The disadvantages of the Matrix approach include:

- Difficulty managing many Matrix price points and keeping them in sync with the market as conditions change. If not well managed, Sales will have little confidence in a product's price points in each matrix.
- Over time, the majority of the revenue may become concentrated in just a few matrices, which results in pricing that is under-differentiated and produces lower margins than intended.
- Customer assignment to a group is generally subjective but may have some objective qualifiers which need to be reviewed periodically.
- There is a tendency to create a new matrix to solve a pricing problem, which creates many ad hoc solutions.

The obvious advantages of a well-managed Matrix approach include:

- There are fewer customer specific agreements to maintain—multiple customers share the same pricing. This balances the time and effort to manage lots of accounts that don't justify a manually intensive approach.
- The company has the ability to define the price matrices as a discount off "The" List Price, which facilitates sales communications in some industries.
- There is flexibility and ease in responding to new market initiatives.

Regardless of whether your company believes a Negotiated price approach, or a Matrix price approach makes the most sense, you can use micro-market price segmentation to inform and improve the price setting and ongoing management process. Visually, how can we represent "The" List Price and Matrix **"pricing vehicles"** and their scope?

Sometimes it's appropriate to think of "The" List Price as the publicly visible, customer-anonymous, internet or web price. You know nothing about the potential buyer until after the fact. There is never any negotiation in this type of sale. Set the price too high and they walk away. Set the price too low and you leave money on the table. Either way, **you spill fuel on the track**.

As part of any Matrix Price approach, you will know *something* about the potential customer, such as twelve months spend, customer industry/ vertical, geographic data, customer's breadth of business with your company, etc. These customers are not a black box because you know their identity and have placed them in, or they have elected to be placed in, some marketing tier or group, or some similar program that entitles them to buy from your company at some pre-determined, but reduced price (vs. "The" List Price).

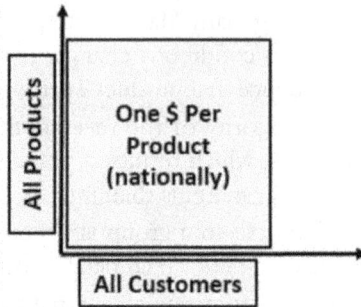

Chart 9 - 'The' List Price and Scope

Instead of one List Price, there are multiple price lists based on some product hierarchy levels and some grouping of customers. The groupings are based on your company's valuation and assignment of those customers into structured groups. But because all customers in a structured group are NOT actually as similar as one might like—they just meet certain business driven rules – the true price sensitivities for each product on those matrix price lists can vary significantly, customer to customer.

In a well-constructed design, the Matrix Price aims to drive greater market price differentiation providing distinct pricing for relatively balanced fractions of revenue, see Chart 10, for the affected products. Unfortunately, over time, some price lists will become much more heavily utilized than others, and some periodic reassessment and redefinition is needed to maintain market price differentiation for certain products.

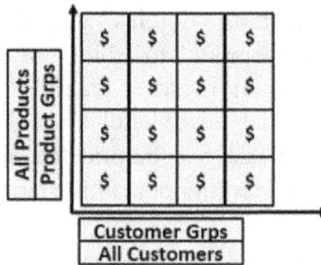

Chart 10 - Structured Matrix Prices and Scope

Filling the matrix price lists with $ signs for actual volume, we would hope they would have similar counts of $ signs. However, when we do this, we often find something like Chart 11. We see that some matrix prices are heavily used, and others seldom used. In this example, your company may believe it has 16 distinct prices in the market for a product, but you may find your market is actually under differentiated. This is because really you are using only 5 price points with significant frequency and 2 price points not at all.

While a Price Matrix approach can help you manage numerous customers by allowing them to share the same price lists, keeping customers aligned onto the right price lists requires a periodic review. When product pricing is under differentiated, then by definition you are **spilling fuel on the track!**

As mentioned earlier, a concern with Matrix Pricing is the ease with which new price lists can be created or changed. The result is that over time, a company's carefully crafted matrix in Chart 11 can evolve into one like Chart 12. Issues can include in "holes" in the matrix, customers being aligned poorly, and some customers being able to buy from multiple matrices, which allows for cannibalization within your own pricing—which only makes it very possible to **spill fuel on the track!**

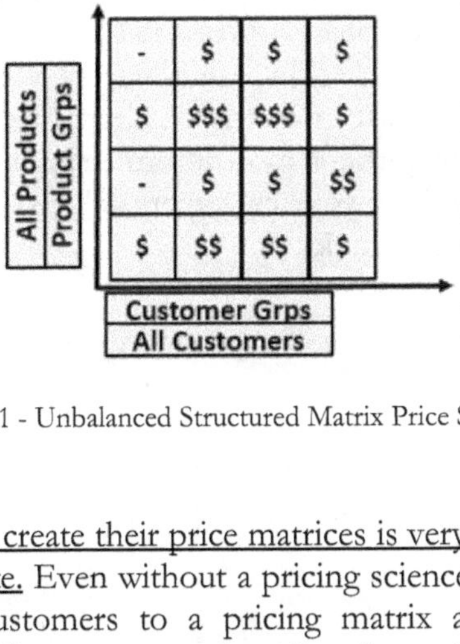

Chart 11 - Unbalanced Structured Matrix Price Scope

How companies create their price matrices is very important, and typically it is not very deliberate. Even without a pricing science approach, if companies deliberately assign customers to a pricing matrix and then enforce those assignments, they will reap some benefits from this better management. **Typically, a price matrix assignment can be made based on three very general considerations:**

1. **Customer demographic**—this represents some inherent customer attributes that are very stable over time, such as industry, channel, or geography.

2. **Customer election**—this allows the customer to have input and commit to some behavior for some benefit, such as free shipping for orders greater than $X or certain payment terms.

3. **Customer performance assignment**—this includes factual attributes, such as rolling 12-months spend or portfolio breadth of support or account health or similar.

Unless these customer price matrix assignments are well managed and enforced to keep them from being frequently and unjustifiably changed, the resulting revenue (and profit) dollars will look like Chart 12, not Chart 10.

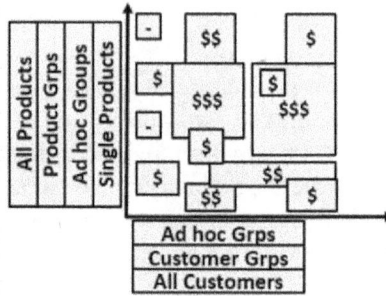

Chart 12 - Unbalanced Matrix Price Scope

To summarize, there are pros and cons to "The" List Price, Matrix Price, and Negotiated Price approaches. But using 'science-y' techniques to improve how your company sets its List or Matrix or Negotiated prices will help drive greater price differentiation through more informed segmentation. This will give you the most insight into how your customers will respond and minimize the chance you **spill fuel on the track.**

Chapter 4
The Big Picture

Look at market fluctuations as your friend
rather than your enemy; profit from folly rather than
participate in it.   Warren Buffett[13]

In an operational environment, "success" in price setting and negotiation means accomplishing your company's over-arching pricing objectives. Whether your goal is maximizing margin or maximizing revenue or some blend, you must be able to manage your **pricing vehicles** and effectively respond **without spilling fuel on the track**. Your pricing objectives must be intimately tied to the company's strategic objectives. Racing from pricing event to pricing event without a clear picture of how your activities fit into the over-arching pricing and strategic company objectives simply increases your workload and increases the chance that you are mispricing opportunities.

In many B2B markets, most revenue frequently comes from agreements of some sort. These may be formal contracts, or they may simply be understood to be pseudo-binding deals— in other words, non-spot market transactions. Pricing deals of any sort are made at a point in time for specific sets of products, often with an assurance of volume from the buyer, but no guarantee. And very importantly, this pricing can stay in force for years.

A key challenge is managing agreements and keeping the pricing current. Over the course of the last 30 years delivering data-driven pricing solutions, I have found multiple customer agreements containing price lines with effective dates over 10 years prior.

Sometimes their costs had decreased significantly, and the companies were quite happy to have a customer willing to pay an exceedingly high price. In the other cases, their costs had increased dramatically, and **they were spilling fuel on the track every lap** (on each transaction) and did not know it.

A typical agreement might include tens to hundreds of products, and then manually pricing an agreement can be a very inefficient and arbitrary process. This inefficiency is generally driven by the number of products and a negotiation duration period, which can be days to weeks to complete. So, price setting is usually a resource constrained problem.

Last, and most importantly, in most cases the final pricing decisions are made by the Sales Rep, so it's a challenge to **give the negotiator actionable pricing guidance before the price is agreed to**—which is essential to **stop leaking profit!** This is why a business intelligence tool approach is most useful for finding unprofitable, unintentional outliers, but only after the fact.

Alternatively, an algorithmic approach can proactively provide pricing guidance via price negotiation ranges. A 'science-y' algorithmic approach helps turn big data into information, and information into intelligence, which can be used while negotiating a new agreement or a renewal or change to an existing agreement.

As I mentioned in Chapter 2, I worked with a large electrical manufacturer with different business units which needed to agree on what constituted a long vs. medium vs. short duration agreement. Some might ask why does it matter?

In my view there are three strong business reasons. First, establishing fixed durations for types of agreements prevents things like the 10-year-old prices. Second, defined agreement periods put into sharper contrast the question of who is absorbing the risk. In a longer-term agreement, you should be balancing the margin risk with the potential revenue stream via some mechanism. Depending on your industry, setting price as a fixed dollar amount or a discount from list percentage or tying the price to some public index may be standard practice. Being cognizant of the contract duration is central to managing your risk. Lastly, particular attention needs to be paid to the customer relationship when pricing longer vs. shorter agreements so that you construct wins for both parties.

Core to all the above, to create a "win-win" you must recognize different selling circumstances and price differently. And the main logic at the heart of ERP system modules or simple spreadsheet models is that not all customers value your products the same. It's no surprise that different customers will value your high-end automotive widget "X" differently, and depending on the circumstances there might also be another component—a temporal component.

Over 25 years ago, Bob Cross wrote an illuminating and seminal book on the principles of revenue management.[14] I worked with him at his revenue management firm for five years. Bob used to tell a story about his time with the Texas Aeronautics Commission when he frequently flew to DC to file paperwork with the FAA. What he noted was that some flights were mostly filled with "briefcase fliers."

When he went to work for Delta Airlines several years later, one of his career broadening assignments was to work in marketing. What he knew from experience was that some fliers bought their tickets well in advance and were genuinely concerned with price, while other fliers bought their tickets late and price was not an issue. As he said, if you must testify on short notice at some government proceeding, the price of the ticket is not a factor in your decision. The flier who buys at the last minute is usually much less price sensitive than the flier who buys early. In B2B parlance, the customer that needs the product on short notice is less likely to be a 'price sensitive shopper'—those customers will be more interested in product availability and quick shipment, as well as reliability and dependability.[15]

With that in mind, I view the broadest general types of B2B segmentation as customer attributes, product attributes, and order (including temporal) attributes. Your mindset should be to find all three types of profit leaks and plug them—only reward the right customers, not all customers, with your best pricing. As my good friend and colleague Barrett Thompson often says: "Reward the set of customer behaviors that you want to encourage with more attractive pricing—things like big orders, or long lead times, or broad product mix, or high share-of-wallet, you get to decide this!"

Chart 13 - What is this customer willing to pay today?

Not All Customers Are the Same

Many years ago, UPS had a single price for all its customers because it was "fair." In their minds, "fair" was part of a market positioning formula.[16] But UPS changed their approach after FedEx's swift success, which was in part based on its matrix pricing.

Why did it work? FedEx recognized that certain customers valued some delivery times more than others (e.g., 8AM, 10AM, any time next day delivery, 3–5-day delivery). Customers also valued parcel versus letter delivery differently—it certainly costs little more to carry a small box than a 9×12-inch envelope. Using a national or regional average price for your customer base will almost guarantee you are **leaking fuel on the track.** Some customers will be paying less than the value they receive and perceive.

When I worked for Sprint (now T-Mobile) in their Customer Network Design Center, we built quote-pricing software for the Sales team. I recall a new voice product offering was about to be introduced into the market and after dissecting how it had been designed by marketing, we realized it had a flaw. We had a meeting with the Kansas City marketing team to explain the problem.

Later in my career, part of that meeting resonated more clearly with me. After we voiced our concerns, the marketing product development team explained that the pricing was designed for the national average customer and had three-tiered customer spend discount levels. We pointed out that while Sprint Business Services had thousands of customers, and we were very sure <u>we did not have a single customer that had all the attributes of the national average customer</u>. To make a long story short, the root cause of the problem stuck with me, Marketing was building pricing for a national average customer that did not exist. **National or regional averages are NOT informative in price setting.**

A quite common misconception is that price segmentation and price optimization will probably lead to large increases in the offered price. People fear that customers will react badly because of "sticker shock."

In late January 2001, the New York Stock Exchange converted to decimal pricing—pricing to the nearest 1 cent rather than the nearest eighth or sixteenth of a dollar. The effort intended to create more price points in the market to sell a product (a stock) and make it easier for a buyer and a seller to agree on a price. But what is often not mentioned was the additional outcome.

If you have more price points in the market you serve, you can better maximize your revenue and thus improve commissions. Both my parents were stockbrokers and the move to decimalization stirred lots of family discussion. Both before and after the NYSE switched to decimals, there was extensive public debate of the pros and cons. And even two years later, the SEC discussed a potential change to use five-cent price points to garner better market acceptance because people liked "round numbers."[17] But clearly, this decimalization effort did not result in large price changes up or down. In fact, it made the steps or tiers in pricing much smoother.

Let me illustrate the outcome in another way. You might recall from high school advanced math that the area under a curve can be estimated by packing a large number of narrow rectangles under the curve and then calculating the area of each rectangle. The more rectangles used, the closer the estimate. In Chart 14, we can see that as we increase the number of price points from 1 to 5, we increase the number of rectangles. The boxed areas equal sales. The resulting profit lift comes from two areas: capturing new revenue from lower price point customers you had not been serving, and additional revenue from pricing some existing sales higher. In this pictorial example a more than a 30% increase.

A number of years ago, I worked with a customer that manufactured large backup power sources. Their products were routinely unit priced in the $1,000 to $20,000 range. While pricing to the nearest cent would be possible mechanically, it was not felt to be acceptable in their market.

While developing requirements with this company, they defined a new goal to price to the nearest $25 dollars on large price tag items rather than multiples of $100. This would allow them to incrementally adjust their pricing and not affect the customer's demand.

There is a two-sided question here—would the customer be willing to say "no" if you priced it 5 cents or 1 dollar higher? The reverse question is, would you be willing to walk away from an exceptionally low margin sale over that same 5 cents or 1 dollar unit value?

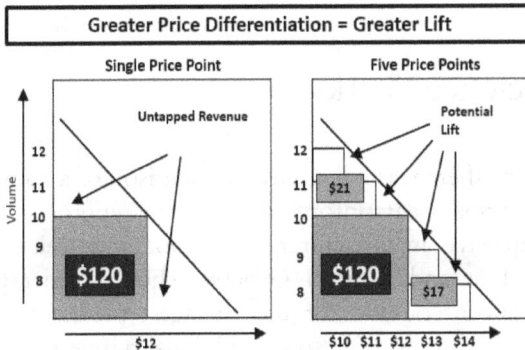

Chart 14 - More Price Points = Greater Lift

A narrow range in price adjustment which does not increase or decrease demand, is **commonly referred to as the "zone of indifference" in pricing**. Using that zone to your advantage is important to getting incremental profit. Different industries have different accepted practices, and various products demonstrate various sensitivities, but typically a price change of 1%-3% will not materially affect a customer's buying habits (for a non-commodity product). In part, this explains the 1/3 to 2/3 "stickiness factor" when companies announce a 5% price increase.

The heart of the matter is elasticity, or price sensitivity, and transactional willingness to pay. Modestly lowering prices will probably NOT stimulate demand from some existing customer segments, but it may allow you to capture a part of the market you may have failed to serve previously.

Let's start with two intuitive examples. If you manufacture fuses and lower your prices, it's not like the fuses know this and then suddenly burn out faster due to your price decrease. Similarly, if you rent apartments and you lower your rents, people do not move out of their houses to rent your apartments.

As my former colleague Brooks Hamilton points out, in many markets, there is some degree of relatively inelastic demand among existing customers because they have fixed procurement programs. If you are not pushing to acquire new customers with the new lower pricing, then all you are doing is pushing a price decrease into your existing customer base, which **spills fuel on the track**.

Some customer types (e.g., automotive repair shops) may switch their purchasing patterns and give you greater wallet share, but other customers are not going to buy 2% more fuses. Assuming you see an increase in demand, what's most likely going on here is you are casting a wider net and serving a new population of customers that you have not served before.

Pricing Science Works

Many years ago, there was a definitive comparison of a company's current pricing approach versus a data-informed, 'science-y' approach. The company was a process intensive manufacturer. The pilot was well-controlled with precisely defined Test and Control Groups. The customer/product/order segmentation scheme accounted for the strongest predictors of price. The market segmentation, coupled with some additional business-informed factors, facilitated calculating reliable price sensitivities in each of hundreds of thousands of price segments.

A 'bake-off' approach was used with the customer implementing an across the board >5% price increase in the Control Group, and in the Test Group selectively implementing various price increases and decreases, price segment by price segment. The goal was to prove the validity of the predicted price sensitivities in each price segment.

The Test and Control groups were selected in such a way that they had similar historical business cycles and purchasing patterns. At the end of the four-month pilot period, the results looked similar to Chart 15.

In the Test Group, some prices were raised and in other prices were lowered so that the revenue weighted average of the price change matched the >5% goal increase. As a result, the Test Group revenue increased significantly.

Group	Avg Price Change 'Stickiness Factor'	Revenue Impact
Test Goal: >5% Average Price Increase	More than 100% of Goal	Sales Increased to >105% of initial
Control (Business As Usual) Goal: >5% Flat Price Increase	About 2/3s of Goal	Sales Decreased to <97% of initial

Chart 15 - Price Sensitivity-Driven Price Increase 'Drag Race'

This was possible because price increases in some segments were over 10% and price decreases in other segments were as much as 3%. But the revenue weighted aggregate price change slightly exceeded the >5% goal price increase and had no overall negative revenue impact.

Some of you might be very skeptical of this result, but experience shows that this is not only possible—raising prices without detrimental revenue impact—but if properly done, it can happen very frequently.

Let me restate this. the Control Group's across-the-board >5% price increase resulted in a stickiness factor of about two-thirds. This one-size-fits-all price increase caused revenue to drop by more than 3%. Why would that be?

An **across-the-board price increase is wrong-headed** because it attempts to treat all customers the same from a price sensitivity perspective.

The problem in the Control Group's business-as-usual approach was that the company essentially 'punished' some customers. High-sensitivity customers and customers paying higher than typical prices relative to their peers received unacceptable increases. Low-sensitivity customers or customers paying low prices relative to their peers received very acceptable price increases and did not complain. The root cause of the imbalance is that the one-size-fits-all approach does not consider the market and a customer's product-specific price sensitivity.

In the Test Group, a price-elasticity-based metric was used to adjust pricing, and we achieved 100%-plus of the price increase goal. We achieved a POSITIVE revenue impact.

In Chart 16 - Multi-Industry Test vs. Control Results, I show some other industry examples where a pricing science has been very effective for driving profitability and revenue growth. These industries are particularly well-suited to reap the advantages of such an approach because they have:

1) A large number of products

2) A large number of customers, and

3) Potentially multiple pricing vehicles for the same product and customers

Test vs Control Price Optimization Impact Summary		
Customer Industry / Type	Margin Lift	Revenue Lift
Automotive Products Distributor	>4%	>4%
Chemicals and Paint Manufacturer	>2%	>8%
Electrical Equipment Manufacturer	>10%	>1%
Equipment Rental Services	>4%	>4%
Food & Beverage Distributor	>10%	>1%
High-Tech / Chip Manufacturer	>13%	>3%
High-Tech / Other Manufacturer	>8%	>6%
Lighting Products Manufacturer	>3%	>3%
Steel & Metals Distributor	>15%	>10%

Chart 16 - Multi-Industry Test vs. Control Results

Now let's turn this scenario on its head. Say your goal is to buy market share in a particular region for some line of products. If you lower prices across the board for all the customer/product/order combinations slightly, you risk giving money away with negligible effect. You may serve some new markets or capture a larger share of some existing customers' purchases. But you will be **spilling fuel on the track** in those segments which are happy with their prior price, and there is no additional demand to capture via the "lower prices."

My usual phrases here are, "allow the customer who is willing to pay more the opportunity to pay more!" and "reward your most desirable customer behaviors with your best prices."

I recently worked with a customer in a business involved in a market suffering from cheaper internationally produced products and a market shift related to e-commerce. This customer wanted to keep existing production facilities operating at nearly full capacity. They asked a typical operationally focused business question, "How much should we reduce price to drive approximately X additional units of demand annually?"

I was able to explain to them that while on average they might reduce pricing by 2.2% and expect to capture the additional demand, in some segments I would recommend no price decrease. This was because price sensitivities indicated a flat response, and they would not likely capture any additional demand, they would just **spill fuel on the track**.

Chapter 5
The New Science of Price Setting

A Practical Solution to an Intractable Problem!

Are you willing to believe that where there's smoke, there's usually fire? Then, in the parlance of this book, if you find high-end engineering, many devoted fans, and lots of high-octane fuel being used, there is probably a car or motorcycle or power boat race in the vicinity.

It should not be a big leap of faith to the open-minded to believe that there is a sturdy foundation underpinning the many "pricing science" storylines. Publications such as CEO Magazine, Forbes, Supply Chain Weekly, The Professional Pricing Society Journal, The McKinsey Quarterly, and Manufacturing Today Magazine, just to name a very few, have all featured such articles. (See the section Appendix 1: Useful References and the End Notes for a broader list.)

A fundamental premise behind big data is that looking at a problem at the right level of detail allows you to see and act on patterns that otherwise muddled in "averages" or happen "infrequently." It is very practical to segment your transactional data based on customer, product, and order attributes and use that to calculate price sensitivities to drive pricing guidance in a repeatable and timely fashion.

Chart 17 lays out the high-level steps which flow from my Seven Keys to Pricing from Chapter 1 Fundamental Ideas. The initial step is getting reliable transactional data from your ERP system and then understanding it. The goal is to discern what it says about customers, products and markets and the strongest price drivers for your customer and products. Most of this is analytical work, but it must also be shaped by a strong understanding of business context.

Once you have determined the strongest price drivers, this forms the basis to segment your transactions, creating many small clusters of transactions that behave the same in "pricing space." By this I mean they share common attributes and have a similar price response (higher or lower). Then through 'science-y' algorithms we can look at each micro-segment of the market to determine the segment's price sensitivity.

Because there could easily be thousands to millions of price segments in your business, this requires an algorithmic approach, not a people-intensive, business intelligence tool approach.

As discussed earlier, how many charts can your analysts realistically look at and decipher? Once you have calculated the price sensitivity in each segment, you have the core that you need to create optimized price negotiation guidance. In summary, in Chart 17, I have depicted the high-level steps:

1. Assemble your transactional data.
2. Organize and statistically analyze the data to find the strongest predictors of price.
3. Evaluate the pricing micro-segments and calculate sensitivities in each pricing micro-segment.
4. Create price guidance that maximizes the probability of closing the deal, while maximizing the business objective of revenue or profit or some mix.

Some of you may already have noticed this, but you should note that the pricing guidance is a range in the lower left corner of the chart — the negotiation

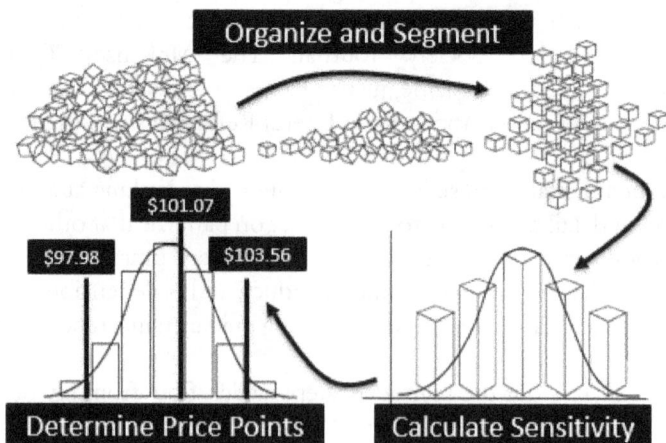

Chart 17 - The Pricing Science Approach

guidance includes a Start price, Target price, and Floor price. What's the point here? Why would we want to provide a range? Why not just provide a profit optimized price and tell the Sales person to get as close as s/he can?

The biggest single reason is that it would be simplistic to believe that everything important about your past transactions was captured in your company's transactional data. In fact, I, like you, know from experience that almost always there will be important deal circumstances that are never captured in the transactional data. Implicit in the optimal price guidance range are all the unrecorded deal factors involved in arriving at the final agreed-to price.

Using this range to guide future negotiation allows your Sales Reps to do what they do best, assess the customer, deal circumstances, and other market intangibles and decide to press higher or not.

The goal of optimized pricing guidance is <u>NOT</u> to replace the Sales Rep, it is to allow them to operate with greater confidence—remember my earlier comments about the "Game of Chicken" in Chapter 2: Pan-Industry Pricing Pain Points.

Chapter 6
People Plus Science
Drive More Profit

How can you **prevent spilling fuel on the track?** Most Sales Reps and product or pricing managers have a good feel for price in the markets they serve on a routine basis—fast moving products sold to larger customers. But Sales Reps benefit from pricing intelligence in three main areas:
1) Selling when they are outside of their usual customer and product zone.
2) Avoiding over discounting when the market is moving up or down.
3) Knowing when two customers/opportunities that seem to be similar really are not.

Because Sales Reps are a competitive bunch, they are also interested to know when someone else has been able to sell at a higher price in a similar circumstance.

Are You Spilling Fuel on The Track?

Let's take a closer look at how this process works. Initially, one might plot transaction line level prices against say customer size and you might get a chart similar to Chart 18, which really says nothing useful. You can't answer the business question, **"Did we spill fuel on the track?"** The price in question certainly looks to be in the midrange of prices for that product and size customer.

By looking for price drivers beyond customer spend, we can develop better

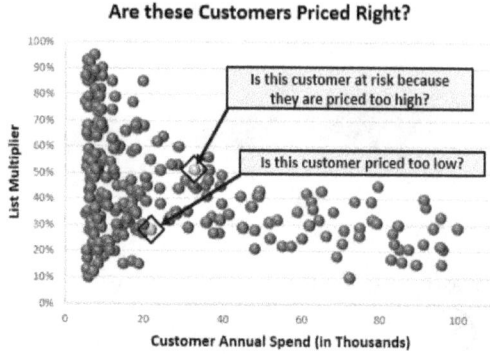

Are these Customers Priced Right?

Chart 18 - Traditional BI Approach without Price Segmentation

insights on what customers have been willing to spend in various micro-segments or small corners of the market. The analytical and business questions of most importance are:

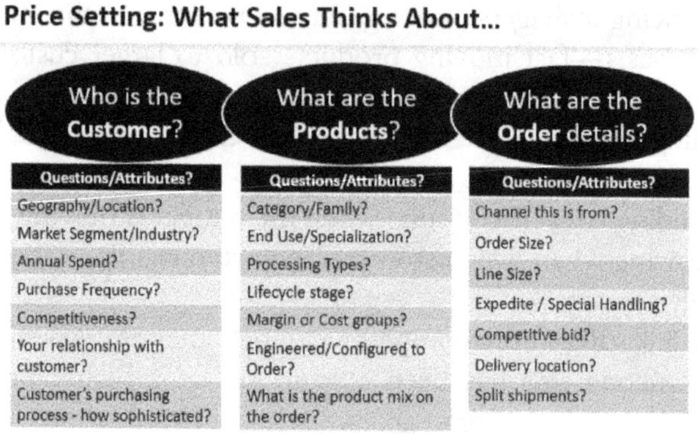

Price Setting: What Sales Thinks About...

Who is the Customer?	What are the Products?	What are the Order details?
Questions/Attributes?	**Questions/Attributes?**	**Questions/Attributes?**
Geography/Location?	Category/Family?	Channel this is from?
Market Segment/Industry?	End Use/Specialization?	Order Size?
Annual Spend?	Processing Types?	Line Size?
Purchase Frequency?	Lifecycle stage?	Expedite / Special Handling?
Competitiveness?	Margin or Cost groups?	Competitive bid?
Your relationship with customer?	Engineered/Configured to Order?	Delivery location?
Customer's purchasing process - how sophisticated?	What is the product mix on the order?	Split shipments?

Chart 19 - Pricing Science and Business Insight

1. What does the Sales Rep think about first, second, third, fourth, fifth, and so on, when they mentally go through their 'pricing as usual' decision making today?

2. What new insights can we gain by looking at the problem algorithmically—What other price drivers can we find, and what did we hear from the Sales team that does <u>not</u> appear to be an important price driver?

Starting with a good understanding of what the Sales team believes is effective in price setting and the available transactional data, we are well positioned to understand new opportunities.

We are looking for combinations of attributes, like the ones in Chart 19, which are highly correlated with either high, low, or middle price points. Some attributes that are highly correlated may be what Sales suggested, and some may not be. Pricing science helps us confirm or discount Sales' suggested attributes as well as uncover new attributes to improve micro-market price segmentation. Finding the best combination of price drivers in the market allows us to predict with a high degree of accuracy the actual middle price point in each of the tens of thousands to millions of price segments.

And, because pricing-science works with transactions from all your company's Sales team, selling to your full array of customers, competing with your full array of competitors, you can understand and determine pricing guidance that is in sync with:

- Which customers and product combinations are more or less price sensitive,
- In which demand streams have you been able to sell at higher or lower margins This inherently captures the effects of geographic, channel, industry and all other competitive responses and pressures,
- Recurring business cycle patterns.

A number of years ago, I had an "old industry" client express to me that for about 4 years they had been dealing with major price pressures, just like today's world. This was because of a variety of factors—recession, transition of business related to e-commerce, and foreign competitors bringing in cheaper products, just to name a few.

This customer was in the midst of a controlled pilot with a Test and Control group. The pricing director heard daily from the field Sales team that one family of products was seeing increasing price pressure. When we reviewed the latest transactional data what we found was that roughly 1/3 to 1/2 of the product family's price segments were continuing to see increased price pressure. Our new price guidance already reflected a lower target price in those segments.

But what was surprising to the pricing director was that in other segments, the Sales team was seeing flat to slightly increasing price points in the latest month's data.

As a result, the price guidance was not lower in those segments. Some Sales Reps were able to sell higher, others were not, based on the region, customer type and other pricing attributes. The new pricing guidance remained "market-aware" and was not lower in those segments.

Without price segment level optimized price negotiation guidance, the human reaction would be to start (or continue) lowering prices in all segments because the only information the pricing director had was the daily calls describing further need to sell lower. No one ever called to tell the pricing director the price was stabilizing or increasing!

What makes a price segmentation attribute a good one? Here are some practical considerations I've found useful over the years:

- Is the attribute known before any price setting/negotiation?
- Is the attribute currently considered by the Sales team when making pricing decisions?
- Does/Will the market accept different pricing based on the attribute?
- Is the attribute data of decent quality?
- Is there some demonstrated moderate to strong correlation with price variability?
- Does the attribute reflect/is the attribute in tune with the business strategy?
- Can the company's IT systems accept such an attribute as a price discriminator?

In Chart 20, I have diagramed one way to illustrate the main ideas behind selecting good pricing attributes to serve as good price predictors. Associated with every transaction, there are several Product attributes, Customer attributes, and Order attributes.

Some of these attributes may be captured in your ERP systems, data

Price Segmentation
3 Broad Types of Attributes Drive Market Prices

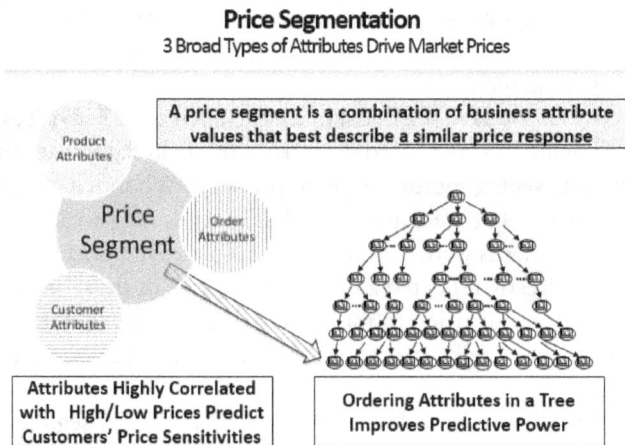

Chart 20 - The Price Segmentation Result

warehouses or quoting platforms, and some other attributes may not be captured explicitly. Determining those attributes and arranging them in a way that maximizes their predictive power is the work of pricing science.

After evaluating the pure transactional data, we often develop some derived attributes that represent business considerations important to the client, but not explicitly present in the data.

For example, some geographic competitiveness metric is usually an important consideration, but there is very, very seldom such a value explicitly on a transaction. Working with these explicit and implicit attributes and using established mathematical techniques, one can determine which of the candidate attributes provide the most powerful prediction of price response and elasticity–which helps businesses to know how their customers respond to price.

About 15-20 years ago, I worked with a lighting customer. Because of the rapidly evolving LED lighting market at the time, an important price setting factor was the type of bulb (fluorescent, incandescent or LED), and for LEDs what technical "generation" of LED. But the market did not care about the generation, it cared about color, lumens, etc., so we created a PLC-like attribute.

The Sales team often talked about this "bulb issue" and a host of other factors including the client's region/country, product brand, Sales channel, Sales territory, market relative competition level, product velocity, deal size, customer predominate product group spend, customer spend level, order line quantity, and job/deal revenue. In short, there was a rather lengthy list of considerations in their business-as-usual mode, and everyone had this in their head.

Using the information on customer, product, and order factors, we dug into the mountains of historical data and developed some key insights. In this case, we saw that product velocity was really a manufacturing/scheduling code and did not accurately reflect sales velocity, so we derived a velocity metric that was helpful.

Likewise, several other factors, like market relative competition level, were not represented in the transactional data. Again, we derived a metric that represented this consideration.

For many other customers, we often find that important pricing factors are not simple one-dimensional metrics (like customer spend). When derived from the available transactional data, these metrics significantly improve price segmentation and elasticity calculations.

At the end of this customer's analysis, we had identified a rank-ordered list of the strongest price drivers. Throughout the price segmentation analysis phase, we worked with the customer to agree on the right mix of business knowledge and scientific insight to create a top-quality price segmentation scheme that be business believed in.

Where Is "The Groove" on the Track?

As mentioned in Chapter 1, an effective price segmentation scheme will group transactions with similar price response together. This makes it possible to determine each micro-market segment's "centerline" price, as well as the price sensitivity within each price segment.

Without getting into the math behind it, I think Charts 21-27 on the next few pages will help you visualize and better grasp on a practical level how this works. The goal here is to answer what I often refer to as the core questions:

- How wide is the highway (the normal range of business in each price segment)?
- How is that normal range of business different for each and every price segment?
  - Remember, price segments are created by analysis of the strongest predictors of high/lower price points in the market
- Where is the dashed-line down the middle of the hi-way?
- How is that center-line different for each and every price segment?

When we plot the unit price versus transaction quantity, we might see a mass of dots that really tells us extraordinarily little about the business. This might look like Chart 21 "All of a Company's Transactions." It looks like this because at this point, there is no price segmentation reflected in the scatterplot. This is where many price analysts resort to gut checks and hunches on what and how to investigate, and this is where pricing science provides a whole new level of insight.

Effectively pricing every one of these opportunities with limited resources would be impossible—you would literally race from pricing event to pricing event with no time to do the required analysis—you would be **racing in a blindfold!** And you would undoubtedly **spill fuel on the track!**

Channel: ALL	Quantity Bin: ALL
Product: ALL	Customer Spend Bin: ALL
Product Sub-Type: ALL	Deal Type: ALL

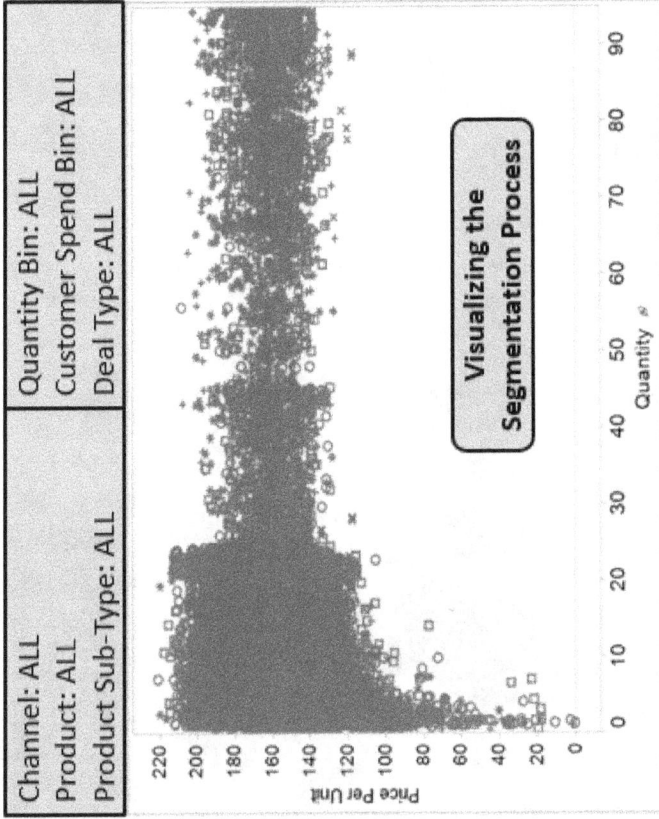

Visualizing the Segmentation Process

Clearly some of the really low-price points at right are not market-driven prices. Those low-priced transactions could be intra-company or employee sales, samples, or associated with some client relationship remedy.

Identifying and handling these cases is important to building a solution that accurately and predictively creates pricing guidance.

Yes, this is real data showing Unit Price vs. Quantity
So can tell me, what is the average selling price?
And does it tell you anything useful?

Chart 21 - All of a Company's Transactions

53

Stop Racing in a Blindfold

When we drill into the pricing using algorithmically determined price drivers we will start to see an increasingly clearer picture

At right we are looking at just one price driver, Channel, and the picture is still very uninformative, as you would expect.

What is the average selling price?
And does it tell you anything useful?

Channel: AAA	Quantity Bin: ALL
Product: ALL	Customer Spend Bin: ALL
Product Sub-Type: ALL	Deal Type: ALL

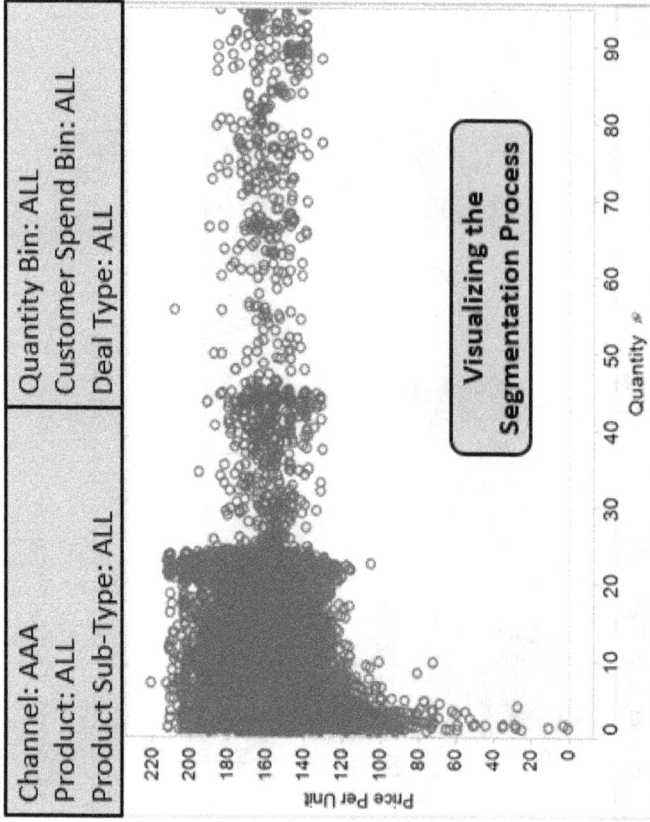

Visualizing the Segmentation Process

Chart 22 - Only 1 Channel's Transactions

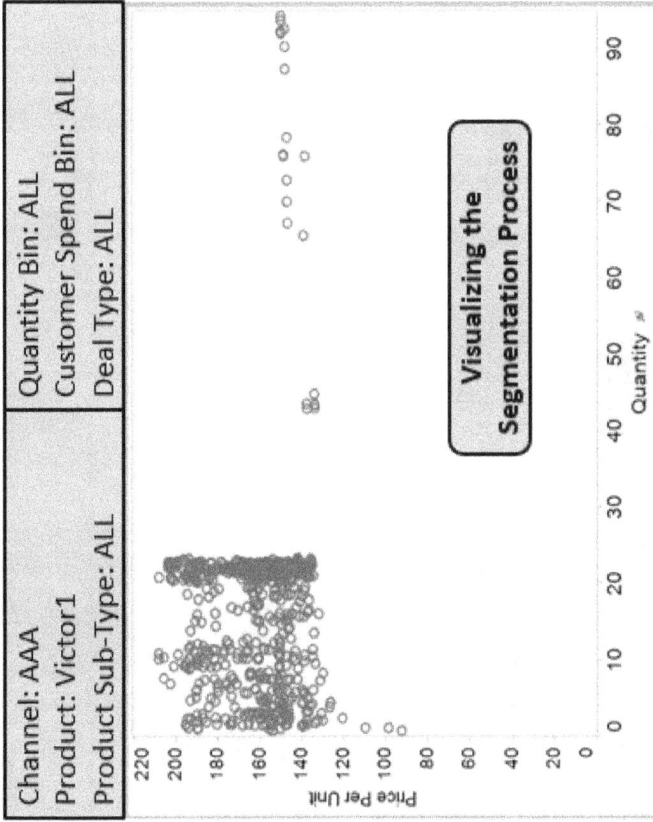

Channel: AAA	Quantity Bin: ALL
Product: Victor1	Customer Spend Bin: ALL
Product Sub-Type: ALL	Deal Type: ALL

Drilling further into the transactions we see the picture is much better, but it seems to have some very odd behaviors – clearly there is a very wide price range for same quantity sales, and vice versa.

At right we are looking at just two price drivers, Channel and Product level, and the picture, is still rather uninformative.

What is the average selling price?
And does it tell you anything useful?

Chart 23 - 1 Channel, 1 Product's Transactions

Stop Racing in a Blindfold

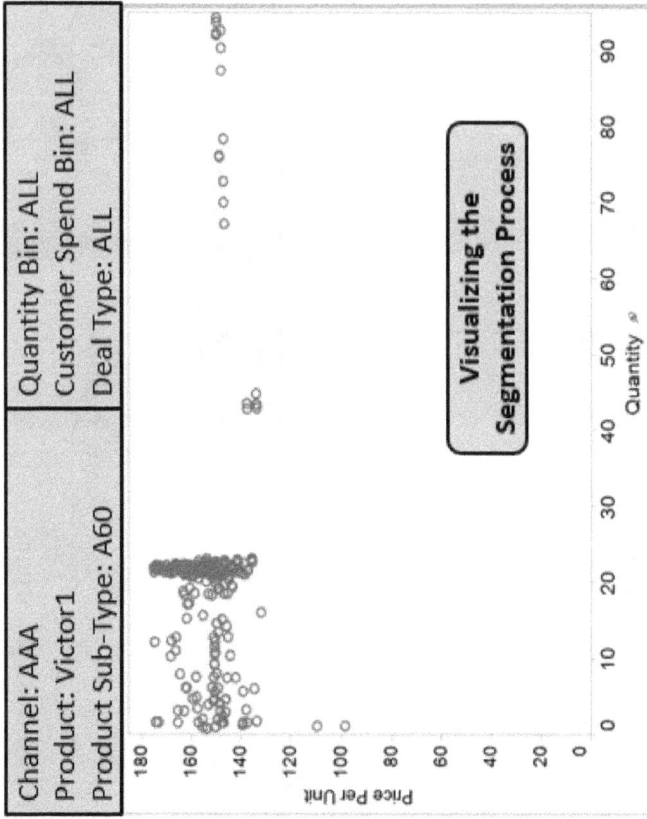

Chart 24 - 1 Channel, 1 Product, 1 Sub Product's Transactions

Drilling down another level we see the picture is a bit clearer, but it seems to have some the odd behaviors we saw before – we still have a very wide price range for same quantity sales, and vice versa.

At right we are looking at just three price drivers, Channel, Product and Sub-product level.

What is the average selling price?
And does it tell you anything useful?

Channel: AAA	Quantity Bin: Large
Product: Victor1	Customer Spend Bin: ALL
Product Sub-Type: A60	Deal Type: ALL

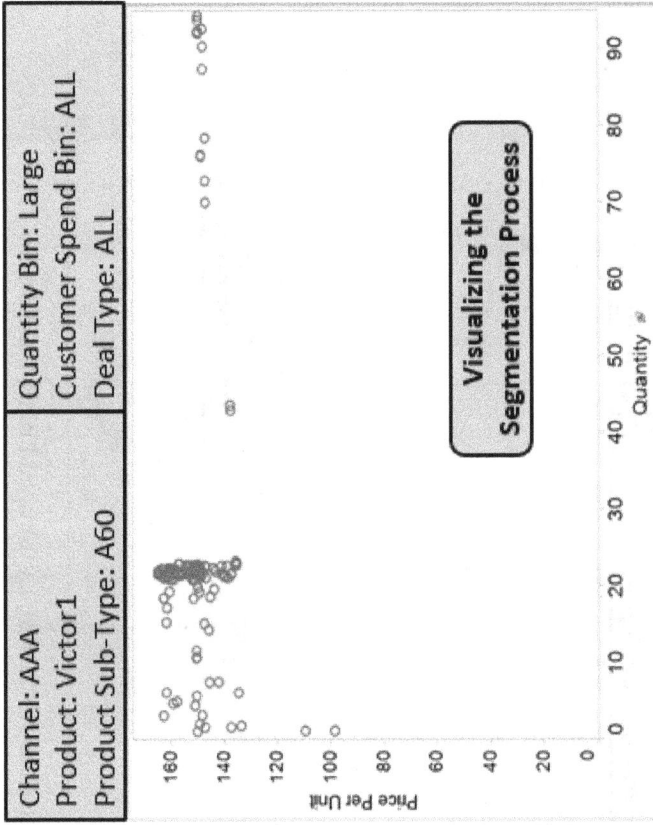

Visualizing the
Segmentation Process

Price Per Unit

Quantity

Adding Quantity Bin to the segmentation and looking only at Large Quantities we see some more improvement, but as before there are still some strange transactions – we still have a very wide price range for same quantity sales, and vice versa.

At right we are looking at just four price drivers, Channel, Product, Sub-product level and Quantity Bin.

What is the average selling price?
And does it tell you anything useful?

Chart 25 - 1 Channel, 1 Product, 1 Sub Prod, 1 Quantity Bin's Transactions

Stop Racing in a Blindfold

Adding Customer Spend Bin to the segmentation and looking only at Large Quantity, High Spend we see some further improvement, but we still have a very wide price range for same quantity sales, and vice versa.

At right we are looking at five price drivers: Channel, Product Sub-product level, Quantity Bin and Spend Bin we can see we are getting close, but we are not there yet.

What is the average selling price?
And does it tell you anything useful?

Channel: AAA	Quantity Bin: Large
Product: Victor1	Customer Spend Bin: High
Product Sub-Type: A60	Deal Type: ALL

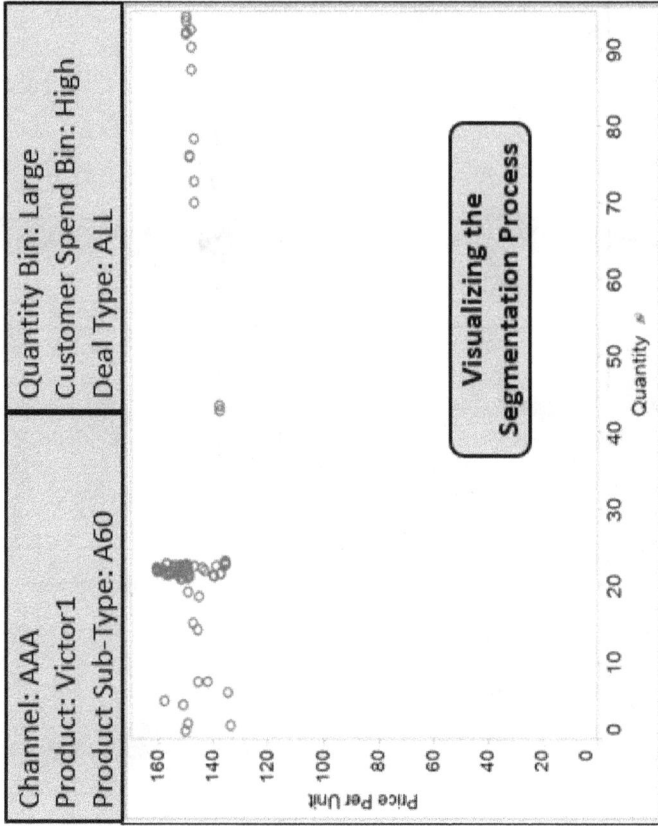

Visualizing the Segmentation Process

Chart 26 - 1 Channel, 1 Product, 1 Sub Prod, 1 Qty Bin, 1 Cust Spend Bin's Transactions

Channel: AAA	Quantity Bin: Large
Product: Victor1	Customer Spend Bin: High
Product Sub-Type: A60	Deal Type: Spot

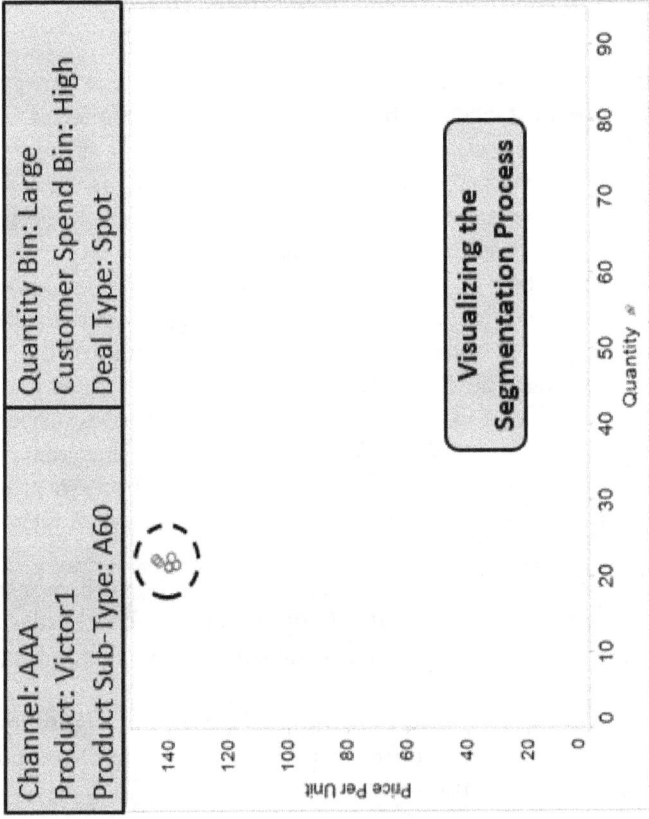

Price Per Unit

Quantity

Visualizing the Segmentation Process

Finally, when we add Deal Type to the segmentation and look at Spot Market/One-Time opportunities we get a very clear picture of the market for this set of specific conditions.

The remaining cluster of circled transactions has a very similar price response to the identified price drivers.

And of course, everyone will look at this picture and say, "gee, that's obvious." If only life were always so simple!

What is the average selling price?
About $140 per unit
Is this insight useful? Absolutely!

Chart 27 - Fully Price Segmented, a Cluster of Transactions

Pricing science can make life simpler. It's pretty clear where the 'groove' is on track for the circumstance in Chart 27 Fully Price Segmented, a Cluster of Transactions. It's also very clear there was no obvious answer at the start.

There is a distinct small range of price versus quantity that is viable in this final micro-segment of the market. The operational pricing challenge is this: could your pricing managers define pricing intelligence at this level of granularity in advance (with perhaps tens or hundreds of thousands of other cases like this one)? Could they keep them all current? Could your company get that pricing intelligence to the negotiator before the next price negotiation? It's the "Right price, Right Customer, Right time!" problem.

The answer is no, they can't. The practical solution is to use 'science-y' algorithm techniques to do this *and more!* We know from experience that getting the pricing intelligence-based guidance to the negotiator with no extra effort on the negotiator's part is also very do-able with some relatively simple integration into your existing quoting platforms.

In Chart 28, you can readily see that there appears to be no demonstrated price sensitivity to quantity. There is little, if any, pattern to how this customer priced larger versus smaller orders (the larger the circle, the greater the revenue in the transaction).

But, when looking at the same data through the lens of algorithmically derived price drivers, we will see a different picture. Fairly often, we find that historical pricing execution just does not make much sense.

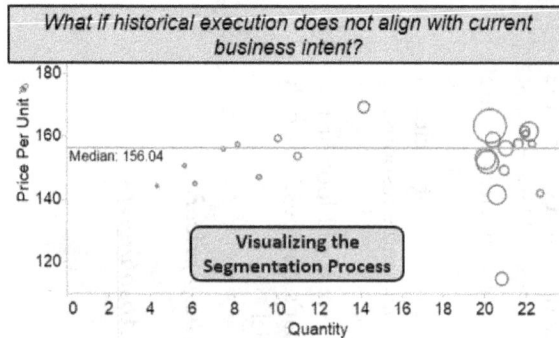

Chart 28 - Bad Historical Business Practice, No Pattern

In comparing Chart 28 to 29, you can see two main points:
1) A coherent pricing approach is probably desired to correct for historically poor business execution that was not in sync with business objectives and common sense!

2) Any approach needs to determine price sensitivity in each price segment. This sensitivity is represented in the second chart via customer spend. In most industries, the business reality is that large customers are more price sensitive to price increases than small customers and will push back harder on price increases.

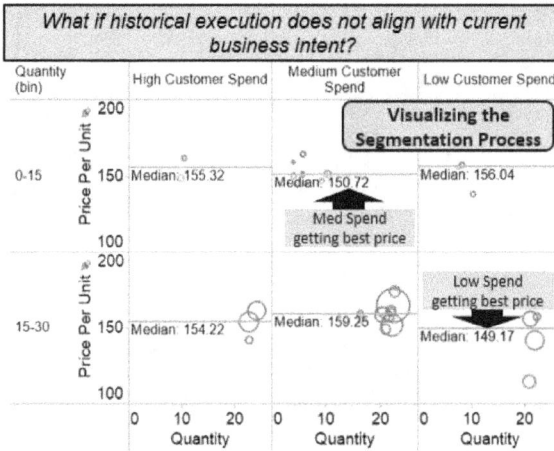

Chart 29 - Segmentation Illuminates How to Correct for Bad History

One should also recognize that an ad hoc, after-the-fact, "rear-view mirror" visual analytics-only approach to pricing can't prevent this misalignment, but it is easy to handle in a repeatable, algorithmic approach. Such an approach can develop pricing guidance to make Sales Reps more effective, because they are smarter about what price range to negotiate in under differing circumstances.

Let's look at the two highlighted panels in Chart 30. But first a little 'chartology.' The panels show the number of transactions (on the vertical axis) that occurred at each price point (on the horizontal axis). You can see how often the company sold each product at each price point in a micro-segment of the market. As seen in both cases, the most frequently occurring prices are in the $148-$160 range.

Looking at Chart 30, most of you would likely conclude that while raising the negotiating range on the left may cause some decrease in quantity demanded, whereas for the one on the right, there would be a much more abrupt drop off in quantity demanded above a certain point. While the optimal price for both is in the $148 to $160 range, it seems the manufacturer has been grossly underpricing the market rather frequently for

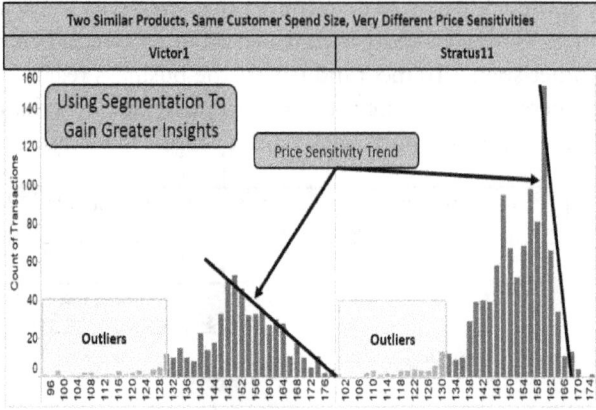

Chart 30 - Segmentation Identifies Clear "Bottom Feeder" Outliers

both products. The long tails to the left reflect how bad this has been by noting the low agreed-to price points, especially the "Outliers" below $130.

In my experience, the key points here are that any algorithmic approach must be able to account for factors as shown in Chart 31, as well as product velocity, geographical considerations, temporal conditions, and other more obvious business-driven differentiators.

Product Victor1	Product Stratus11
Lower Price Sensitivity	Higher Price Sensitivity
Less Price Negotiation (in general)	More Price Negotiation (above a point)
Customers willing to pay higher prices	Customers less willing to pay higher prices
Lots of "outliers" = Lots of opportunity to increase margins by better managing low price points	Lots of "outliers" = Lots of opportunity to increase margins by better managing low price points

Chart 31 - Example Conclusions from Outlier Results

Winning!

The good news here is that given today's pricing science capabilities, it is practical to handle these types of problems and complexities and many more. Rather than trying to handle this via some visual analytics/business intelligence report-driven, ad hoc analysis approach in a Pricing or Sales team support organization, <u>you can lessen the manual workload and improve pricing and profitability</u>. The information is already contained in the historical big data that your business has been gathering. The knowledge of how to turn that transactional data into actionable pricing intelligence is well established and can be applied in a repeatable, algorithmic approach that enables Sales to be smarter and more effective when negotiating.

New strategic business objectives and changing market conditions can also drive a company to want to price differently in the future than how they have priced in the past. As discussed in Chapter 4, being able to leverage your transactional big data archives to drive future objectives is now practical. With an approach like the above, **your company can steer your race car** toward a heavily revenue focused (market growth) objective or a heavily profit focused (margin rate) objective[18] while minimizing the risk of spilling fuel on the track.

The key relationships illustrated in Chart 32 are:
1) There is a price in <u>each micro-segment</u> that will maximize your revenue,
2) There is a price in <u>each micro-segment</u> that will maximize your profit,
3) Selling to the left <u>or</u> right of the revenue and profit "hi-way" means you are leaking both revenue and profit,
4) A key objective must be to keep your pricing in <u>each micro-segment</u> on the pricing "hi-way."

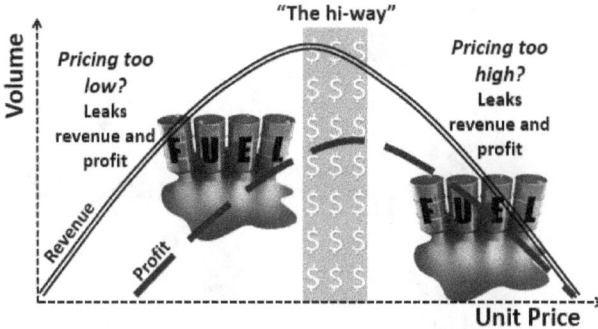

Chart 32 - Strategic Intent - Revenue Growth vs. Profit?

Any long-term, viable pricing process needs to be integrated with business imperatives; the pricing process needs to support the strategic goals of the company. For example, your P&L owner might say "grow market share in product family X in the southern California region," or "stop or reverse margin erosion in channel X in the Chicago area." From Chapter 1: "…*My goal is to help you accomplish your job, close the deal, minimize the chance you left money on the table, and respond to strategic initiatives to improve margins or buy market share…*"

Chapter 7
Some Pricing Complications

This chapter presents five short topics to give you some thought-provoking insights on the broader applicability of an algorithmic, pricing science-based approach in dealing with a very few specialized pricing topics. My goal here is not to delve deeply, but just to introduce a few ideas and experiences.

What's the Value of a Transaction?

One of the rare constants in life is that things frequently change. I often hear in my conversations with Sales Reps and Managers and Pricing Analysts that it's really hard for them to believe that looking at the last 12-24 months of data really has much value from a price setting point of view. Their business may have seasonal patterns, have competitors running different campaigns, or have cost changes all the time. Their company or their competitors may have had supply disruptions, and the list goes on and on and on. It can be a difficult conversation to get them to believe that a price from nine months ago has much to do with next week's market.

The obstacle here is that almost everyone is thinking about the absolute value of each transaction. "A $20/unit price from 9 months ago does not tell me much about the current market" seems like a pretty reasonable comment. But what is important is determining the **relative value of transactions**, not the currency priced value.

Clearly, some transactions are more valuable to your company than others. As mentioned in Chapter 1: Fundamental Ideas, the goals of price segmentation are to group the transactions into small segments that:

- Minimize the price differences within micro-segments,
- Maximize the price differences between micro-segments,
- Provide a basis to calculate price sensitivity within each micro-segment.

When we evaluate price variation, we must make it less "noisy." <u>We want to get at the variation of the true value of the transaction to your business and measure that price response</u>. So how can you do this? There are a few common ways to account for the changes in the market and other factors, but they all revolve around changing the measure of a transaction value from an absolute to a relative metric.

If you divide the transaction unit price by a reference value (for instance, transaction unit price divided by unit cost) you get a better metric for value. To illustrate, if you sold a product for $20 with a cost of $10 in channel A and again with a cost of $15 in channel B, one transaction was obviously more valuable. You'd want to sell more at $20 in channel A than in B.

Similarly, if you have a market index that is updated weekly or monthly, it will allow you to de-trend your up and down historical transactions over time. Last, you might use a List or a comparable price as your reference value.

Being able to discern the relative value of transactions from differing channels, regions, or customer types is critical to evaluating where you should try to make changes in your business. Obviously, you want to grow your business where you are creating the most value for your company.

Most of my clients use a unit cost or list price as a reference value. But let's be clear, using cost as the mechanism to de-trend your transactions and find their relative value does NOT mean you are creating a cost-plus pricing environment. This is just a mechanism for understanding relative value of historical transactions. This allows you to compare transactions that occurred at differing points in time and across different channels or other aspects of your business to ascertain their relative values. We can use those relative transaction values as inputs to the profit optimization.

What's the Real Product You're Pricing?

Assemblies, highly configured, engineered-to-order or made-to-order products pose a special pricing challenge. When you don't have any specific "products" that you sell, or what you sell is frequently custom configured for each client, some would say that price segmentation will simply provide no insight because almost no SKU is sold repeatedly. In my experience that is NOT the case. I am aware of many science-driven pricing solutions for clients that make customer specific versions of plastic bags, O-rings, paper, boxes, glass, electrical equipment, IT components, coatings, mixes and more.

In many cases there is no single SKU that is regularly sold over and over, but the components that go into each product are sold often. When you look at the transactions, you see a jumble of data that may include fields for materials/components, assembly/processing, shipping/packaging, and other charges to the buyer. As an example, one might create a structure like the following to better analyze and understand pricing for components of customized IT products:

- Top Level Category
  (Displays, Computers, Networking, etcetera)
- Functional Use Component Segment
  (Plug Assembly, Disk Stack, Spindle, etcetera)
- Predominant Material Category
  (Plastics, Metal, etcetera)
- Product Material Proportions Groups
  (< 20% copper, <40% copper, etcetera)
- Product Footprint Groups
- Product Thickness Groups
- Product Generation Groups

The trick here is decomposing the plethora of pricing elements into a price stack, where some of those elements can be readily optimized and some probably cannot and need simply to be managed more effectively.

As Chart 33 on the next page depicts, many companies view the quoting process as a mechanism to quote a single line-item price. They typically focus on just the product, and all the other elements of price, like processing, freight, packaging, special handling, special charges, and others don't get much attention. The first step is figuring out which parts of the total unit price can be handled through segmentation and optimization, and what parts need to be better managed as a pass-through or estimate.

Let's say you make plastic bags of varying thickness and dimensions with custom lettering on them and 90% of your sales are for custom bags. How could you price optimize that? Finding a relationship (or creating one) between the market prices you charged, and the amount of material used in the bag could be the core element of the pricing solution, rather than using the final dimensions of the bag. And maybe the lettering or other features are a pure pass-through cost that you manage. Trying to include the total unit price in the model would not work.

The 'Typical' Price Stack

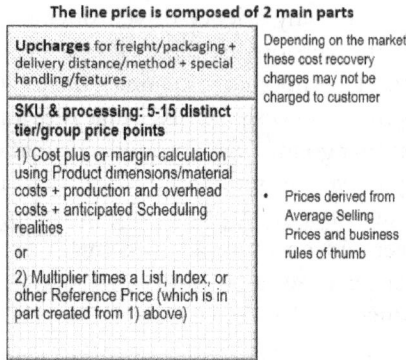

The line price is composed of 2 main parts

Upcharges for freight/packaging + delivery distance/method + special handling/features	Depending on the market these cost recovery charges may not be charged to customer
SKU & processing: 5-15 distinct tier/group price points	
1) Cost plus or margin calculation using Product dimensions/material costs + production and overhead costs + anticipated Scheduling realities or 2) Multiplier times a List, Index, or other Reference Price (which is in part created from 1) above)	• Prices derived from Average Selling Prices and business rules of thumb

Chart 33 - The Price Stack View of Pricing – Before

Similarly, you may be in the business of making custom glass shower doors which you etch and grind. Everything is custom, so no two products repeat. Finding a relationship between the core component elements and some portion of the invoice line price involves breaking the "total" unit price problem into parts. This is what I've called a price stack in Chart 33, the 'Typical' Price Stack

The 'Pricing science' Price Stack

The line price is composed of 3 main parts

Applied at time of price quote	**Upcharges** for freight/packaging + delivery distance/method + special handling/features	Depending on the market these cost recovery charges may not be charged to customer
	Adjustment factors for conditions that can't be readily segmented (business objective driven)	Seasonality, inventory conditions, other infrequent combinations
	SKU: 50-5000 distinct price points	• Known product, customer, and order attributes which have been segmented
	By decomposing the historical transactions to determine how each micro-market valued the 'material only' product	
	Produce segment specific, Optimal Price Guidance	• Segment prices derived from segmentation and elasticity

Chart 34 - The Price Stack View of Pricing – After

(the As-Is State) and Chart 34 The 'Pricing science' Price Stack (the Future State) respectively.

Using this approach, a line-specific price can be assembled <u>at time of quote</u>. In the prior bag example, we can optimize the price elements associated with material and process components. Once the optimal guidance is available, then the order specific differences can be layered onto the price stack—in this case maybe printing charges, freight delivery charges, or seasonal adjustment factors.

In summary, some parts of the price stack components are fully segmented and optimized, while other parts may be estimated (because they can't be known at the time of quote) and other parts are priced as a pass-through (with or without some fixed markup). By decomposing the problem, you can optimize the appropriate parts of the pricing and better manage the remainder.

Who's Paying for Freight?

Do your customers always pay you for freight, or do you sometimes 'eat' some or all the distribution expense? If your company offers to pay for some or all of the delivery expenses, does that lead to larger orders that are more profitable overall? (Does <u>anyone</u> know?)

Regardless of whether you price freight as a separate line item on a quote or invoice or roll the freight expense into the unit prices quoted, there is room to improve how you price the freight component. In the prior sub-topic, I assumed the status quo on freight, meaning whether your company has managed freight as a pass-through of none or some or all of freight expenses would continue in the future state.

About 4-5 years ago I worked with a client that had lots of truckload charges and shipped product daily from a very large number of production locations to many markets. Some of their customers wanted a delivered price in their agreements. By applying a simple pricing science approach, we were able to create a very useful weekly process that consumed the last 150 days of delivery costs and produced a recommended per piece freight charge based on each piece's weight. This allowed them to put data to work for them and **stop leaking fuel on the track!**.

But maybe your CEO has a new intent in the future—maybe it's simply to decrease your freight losses. Or, maybe the intent is to charge more for freight more often and convert an expected loss into a profit center. Thinking about the earlier price stack discussion, in many industries, delivery freight expenses can be a major cost-to-serve element. If through segmentation and optimization you could price this delivery expense to be less of a cost and more of a profit in some cases, this should be of interest! Has this been done? The short answer is yes, we have done this.

Analysis and segmentation are again the key to finding out which customers may be willing to pay more of the freight costs, and then pricing freight to those customers in order to improve overall profitability.

My thoughts here are **"allow the customer who is willing to pay more the opportunity to pay more!"** and "reward your most desirable customer behaviors with your best prices."

A recent client allowed customers to opt for a landed price or a 'product only' unit price with a separate line on the invoice for freight. But many companies just absorb a large fraction of the delivery costs. While this is often framed as "industry practice," truly little thought has gone into how much of the freight expense they could get customers to pay under certain circumstances. As a result, **these companies are spilling fuel on the track!**

Several years ago, I worked with a client that was using a two-year-old paper document as the basis for all freight estimates. They had no process for even considering whether it made sense to get their customers to pay more of the freight expenses. The good news is they had larger than average profit improvement opportunities!

What's the Right Size of a Rebate?

Around 12 years ago, I worked with a client to devise a rebate segmentation and optimization solution. This was a large national distributor that sold many products from an even larger number of manufacturers. Those manufacturers paid the distributor to service their clients on their behalf. The novel question posed was, "Could the price-segmentation approach be adapted to help the distributor justify larger rebates from some manufacturers under various circumstances?"

Look back at the first special topic and review the segmentation goals. Clearly, if one can find attributes that are well correlated with higher or lower rebates and create clusters with a similar 'price' response, then it would be very feasible—and in fact, it was. We used end customer attributes like size and volume and location, coupled with other product information, purchase frequency data, and other attributes. This approach allowed creating a solution that helped the distributor put some "big data" logic behind their requests when they felt the offered product rebates were below average for similar circumstances.

Expanding this idea to handle the reverse perspective is equally interesting. For large manufacturers that employ a rebate strategy through a variety of distributors, the operative question is, "How much should we be paying each distributor to service various customers based on the products and frequency with which those end customers buy?"

While some might argue that a certain class of end customers warrants a product specific rebate regardless of the distributor (or location or other considerations), understanding the price drivers of the situation will make the manufacturer smarter when defining a rebate for a distributor. Realizing this helps **reduce the chance you will spill fuel on the track.**

When we described the original approach at a large conference, there were several manufacturers that expressed concerns that this distributor could use that solution to negotiate better rebates from them—it would raise their costs! But after some discussion back and forth, both groups of clients agreed that understanding where the manufacturer was underpaying or overpaying on rebates was key to both the distributor's and the manufacturer's efforts to improve profitability.

What's a Good Controlled Pilot?

Running a true pilot is really a 'science-y' drag race. Many people will call something a pilot, but unless you are conducting a well-designed test, one that plans for and accounts for things like market fluctuations and changes in buying patterns, it is hard to draw any firm conclusions. You'd be closer to launching weather balloons than running a meaningful pilot.

So much can change between the start and the end of the pilot that if you don't plan for this in your design, your hoped-for clear conclusions will likely be muddled. There are several key thoughts here, and people have written whole books on Test versus Control, so I'll just talk about some very basic ideas.

First, drawing firm conclusions that both the customer and I can agree on is paramount—else, why bother? Drawing firm conclusions enables my clients to extrapolate the results to the larger market or business. To make this possible, we must define two "comparable groups." There are several ways to design and select "comparable groups," but as a minimum they need to have roughly similar revenues and margin levels over time, and they need to have a comparable product mix, similar customer sizes, and similar numbers of customers. This is crucially important to minimize the chances that some "whale" transaction or some other exceptional business event has an undue effect on one group during the pilot.

Typically, I discuss the concept of being able to identify success using Chart 35. The two groups need to be assessed in a baseline period to determine whether they have been performing similarly. Then, during the pilot or measurement period, when new pricing guidance is introduced only to the Test Group, the same two groups are again measured using the same metric. Certainly, there will be differences in the business between the two groups during the pilot period. But because of the intentional design approach to create as comparable-as-possible groups, the market noise is accounted for, and we will see the market response to the new pricing.

Four cases the pilot design must handle to drive good analysis

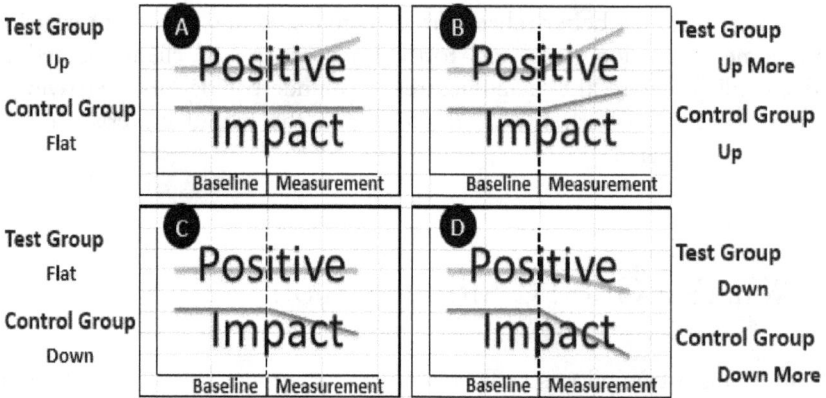

Chart 35 - Pilot Design Cases

Lastly, we need a simple to understand success metric, one that can be stated like this: *The Test Group will show a minimum X% better margin rate during the measurement period when compared to the Control Group.* With a clear definition of what success looks like, it is very clear how use the four cases in Chart 35 to show that the Test Group outperformed the Control Group, or that it did not.

Chapter 8
Bringing It All Together

...the companies with the most pricing power use technological tools to measure value and willingness to pay in a systematic way. They let evidence and facts drive innovation processes. Our study found that the top 10% of companies use pricing software and technology 40% more often than the bottom 90%.[19]
Harvard Business Review Blog Network

The importance of all the solution facets in the prior seven chapters is well illustrated by the following two case summaries, one in a manufacturing industry and the other in a service industry. Your ability to compete and win in each small slice of the market hinges on knowing as much as you can about how your customer will respond to pricing initiatives in <u>that</u> microsegment.

I encourage you to read through these following cases as well as the referenced supplemental material; they illustrate the challenges and the benefits of putting pricing science and big data to work for you. These companies worked diligently to create the pricing levers that helped them **stop spilling fuel on the track.**

Case Summary

Over 15 years ago, we worked with Shaw Industries Group, Inc., a subsidiary of Berkshire Hathaway, Inc. They are the world's largest carpet manufacturer. At the time, Shaw had more than $4 billion in annual sales and approximately 23,000 associates worldwide.[20] Shaw, and the wider carpet industry operates in a complex environment—their customers involve a variety of organizations.

Every quote potentially encountered the conflicting needs of architecture & design firms, dealers, and end users. Additionally, there were differing requirements for "Program" and "Project" purchases, and there were concerns about price differentiation and legal ability to differentiate prices to various customers.

Shaw's markets and competitors are constantly changing. Because of the volatility of petroleum-based products, they experience massive cost changes. Lastly, in 2007 the Sales team was burdened with a lack of good metrics and Shaw's "central pricing organization" only consisted of two people. They were hard pressed to perform new product pricing, and they were also supposed to respond with specific pricing on daily quotes. Since they did not have any time to do things proactively, they were **racing in a blindfold from pricing event to pricing event**.

Shaw's pricing team was responsible at the time for about 5000 SKUs each with over ten price tiers ranging from significantly above to significantly below each product's national average price point. They had a defined Sales Management price approval process that kicked in when the proposed price was below the lowest tier. Historically, over 50% of their transactions were negotiated below this lowest tier price. Sales used "tribal" knowledge to decide on which of the 10+ tier price levels at which to start price negotiations. As with many clients, Shaw's Sales Reps were concerned about:

1) Customer relationship
2) Quote specifics
3) Competition (if any)
4) Size of the opportunity
5) Urgency.

However, there was no defined guidance or consensus on how to relatively weight these factors in any deal opportunity.

Fortunately, Shaw had been involved in a supply chain process improvement effort and understood the value of analytics and metrics in driving decisions. But they lacked meaningful insight into how to apply these skills to a pricing problem. They also realized that with a two-person pricing organization, they could not proactively create pricing for a large Sales team that was requesting many more pricing analyses requests every day than a two person staff could handle. They also knew that an army of pricing analysts would not solve the main issue of how to tap into their "tribal knowledge" and share that with the larger Sales team in a proactive manner.

Because of their early data-driven decision culture, they believed that the best way to prove a pricing initiative was to conduct a controlled Test versus

Control experiment where some group of transactions would receive price negotiation guidance and others would continue with the "business-as-usual approach." They knew they could detect if the price guidance generated margin improvement.

One major challenge was that Sales was literally using paper price books that they carried around with them to determine what pricing was in place for their products. So, how could they possibly get better pricing to their Sales team? The initial segmentation did not dramatically expand the 10+ price points per product. But it created pricing micro-segments using the strongest price drivers, and it considered the relative price sensitivities in each new micro-segment to provide price guidance that was "tuned" to improve profits without putting revenue at risk.

In Shaw's words *"Precision Price Segmentation was crucial for identifying all the specific situations and circumstances where a different price was needed. Sure, we had a strong instinct that Job Size and Competitive Region mattered, but by exactly how much, and did those factors change in their importance as the product category or style changed?"* Solving this price sensitivity problem was one of the major advantages derived from the pricing science segmentation effort.

The resulting new pricing was very explicit and highly specific to the selling circumstances that their Sales Reps encountered daily. By leveraging their historical "big data" transactions, Shaw replaced gut-driven with data-driven factors that influence price. The price segmentation effort and resulting segment level price sensitivity led to actionable price negotiation guidance (pricing intelligence). The pricing science goal was <u>not</u> to create "the number." Rather, the goal was to provide a finely tuned, opportunity-specific type of guidance while still giving Sales Reps negotiation flexibility that was needed to run their business.

By Shaw's own analysis using a revenue weighted aggregate, the pilot proved that Test had outperformed Control by over 300 basis points in aggregate. A collateral benefit was a decrease in the need for exception approvals, from over 50% of all quotes to roughly 25%—even though the initial micro-market price segmentation had only created about 10% more price points.

Better price segmentation, not significantly more, provided price sensitivity driven lift and still allowed them to work from paper price lists initially. Last, because the paper price list was updated monthly without manual intervention, the pricing guidance remained market-aware and provided a viable negotiation window. As a result, Sales Reps were very accepting of the new pricing intelligence. And when polled, 90% showed they wanted to keep the new system rather than the old price tier system.

Because the pilot was well received and increased margins, Shaw then had a case to pursue additional process improvements. Among those initiatives was the adoption of an electronic delivery platform to make the pricing guidance available to Sales in a non-paper form via Blackberrys, tablet computers with remote wireless access, and other tools that gave Sales Reps pricing on demand. Last, they created several new pricing analytics reports to better track and manage pricing achievements and challenges.

After the pilot, the Shaw executive team set new goals to simultaneously grow their market share by revenue and profit dollars. Because of the new pricing segmentation, they could lower prices only where it would produce market growth and raise prices where it would not degrade profitability.

Shaw remains a pioneer in their industry; they were the first in their industry to apply pricing science to their pricing process. They not only have applied pricing science to gain insights into their customers' buying patterns, but they also used optimization to create new pricing guidance, and they have implemented pricing analytics to monitor and report on the effects.

To summarize, Shaw was successful in their pricing initiative because:

1) Shaw knew that further "leaning" the supply chain would produce extremely limited additional profit increases.

2) Shaw knew their existing top down, business rule driven approach was resulting in over half their pricing being below their internal floor price. They also realized that hiring an army of analysts was not a viable solution and that product managers could not manage more of the lifecycle.

4) Shaw knew that their customers valued their products differently, but also knew they could not create and manage more prices manually.

5) Shaw knew they needed better analytics, but they also knew that after-the-fact analytics would not solve their need for predictive pricing guidance.

6) Shaw was aware of the much-touted rule that a 1% price increase typically leads to an 8-11% profit improvement.

Client News Story Summary

United Rentals, the world's largest equipment rental provider, reported in International Rental News magazine[21] in 2011 that it was seeing increasing rental rates and projecting margin rate increases of at least 5%. The article highlights how their new pricing/rate management program works. As CEO Michael Kneeland noted, the program, known as Customer-Oriented Rate Excellence (or CORE) is "...technically enhanced decision-making that gives us price optimization, meaning the proper balance of value for our company and our customers. That may sound aspirational, but it is very achievable for us in the rental environment." The solution produces pricing guidance for each individual customer at the time of transaction using the same approach we have discussed in this book.

Later in the article, Mr. Kneeland says, "CORE has brought consistency to the way we serve customers, and they are appreciative of that. Our branches within a trade area find it easier to work together now, because pricing is set consistently within the market. CORE has greatly reduced the ad hoc manual override of rates in the field."

In closing, Mr. Kneeland states that United Rentals' investment in technology is a game-changer for long-term profitability. "We absolutely believe it is …it strengthens our logistics, our metrics, our margins, and the levers that drive them. **Most of all, it gives our people better information to make better decisions and lets them use the full force of their talents.** [Emphasis added] With CORE, we have state of the art technology, sales reps who believe in the rates, and great feedback. This is a genuine systemic innovation."

I could not have said it better! But I will add one side note, in June of 2011 United Rentals stock price was around $12, and at the end of 2023 it was well over $550. While better market pricing can't take credit for that on its own, it certainly was supportive of efforts to improve company profitability.

Chapter 9
The Leadership Challenge

We've spent a lot of time talking about better pricing, leading to better top-line and bottom-line decisions. We have also talked about how to link pricing strategy, objectives, and tactics to your company's business objectives. But stepping back, I want to share some other observations from years of being a management consultant, business/pricing analyst, and pricing scientist involving many pricing improvement initiatives, and from my many years as a West Point graduate and Army officer leading people and organizations.

Pricing Science is not a Panacea

Foremost, I think it's very important to recognize that not all things that masquerade as pricing problems are true pricing problems. Here are two anecdotes that represent this.

Thirty years ago, Sprint (now part of T-Mobile), had just completed a bid to provide a corporate data network for Sears. Their Customer Network Design Center had labored for months, getting all the data to design and price a data network so that Sears could download its store sales data every night to their corporate mainframes. There was lots of design work to specify the technical requirements. Then even more pricing work went into figuring out how aggressive Sprint could be. Sprint really wanted Sears as a marquee client at that point in time.

This was an exceedingly high visibility bid. Several weeks after the bid was submitted, the two CEOs went to lunch. A few days later, the word came down that the deal was sealed. What the pricing team later learned was that the price point agreed to was not even close to the bid that had been laboriously developed, it was much lower.

The lesson learned was that in the end, this was not so much a pricing problem as it was a business relationship problem. Sprint wanted Sears as a marquee client. Price (and hence deal profitability) was not the primary concern!

There are sometimes very valid business reasons why a company may choose to do business at an exceptionally low price point. With that in mind, a key business advantage flows from price segmentation efforts, price sensitivity calculations, and price optimization. That advantage is that the resulting pricing guidance (pricing intelligence) allows your company to assess what a deal really costs your company in foregone profits. But most importantly, you can prevent inadvertently taking abnormally low-priced business (**leaking fuel on the track**), because the pricing guidance is market-driven and willingness-to-pay sensitive.

Similarly, a few years back, I worked with a paper industry client that ran several paper mills. During some periods of the year, the focus was very much on plant utilization rather than profitability. Paper plants, like petroleum refineries, are a continuous chemical process and shutting down a plant brings significant re-start costs. Plant utilization becomes particularly important in low demand periods. Via price optimization, they gained the ability to quantify the impact of offering incredibly low prices to meet minimum plant utilization goals in some periods versus offering incredibly low prices for no good business reason in other periods of the year.

One last topic, I have had many customers mention or ask direct questions about how to keep employees from "gaming" the pricing system. It's human nature for your Sales Reps to want to close deals and manage their relationship with their customers. In fact, you want your Sales Reps to be active in figuring out how to close a deal.

Several years ago, a large manufacturer described a variation of this where someone might enter a specific order quantity to get it priced as a large order. They believed that people were then later changing the quantity back to a smaller quantity or that the Sales Rep colluded with the customer and knew that the customer would not buy the full quantity quoted.

The customer VP asked how this pricing science approach could protect them against this type of activity. My long-time colleague and friend Barrett Thompson replied "…there is no software solution to an integrity problem." As he explained further, one of the main reasons that analytics are valuable is for measuring customer conformance – Did they do the amount of business they promised you? When that agreement is up for renewal (Do you recall my comments about why defined agreement lengths are useful?), your company can assess whether that customer met its commitments to you in exchange for the pricing that you provided them.

Similarly, being able to find out if your company has groups in your pricing or Sales organizations that have compliance or price realization problems allows you to address those with coaching or development efforts. If you find a "true" integrity problem, something other than a coaching solution is probably appropriate.

At the start of this book, I said that my intent was to help you succeed in pricing in a mid- to high-volume pricing environment. Let's think back about what we have talked about.

In the Shaw and United Rentals cases and other non-attributed examples, we have seen that it is possible to proactively provide market-aware pricing guidance to thousands of quotes a day without an army of pricing analysts. Trying to set top-down pricing rules and manually respond to quotes reduces your market responsiveness. This can lead to a pricing organization that is often viewed as the "sales prevention organization."

While a business intelligence (BI) tool approach is very valuable for gaining insight into the challenges and successes it is experiencing, a BI-only approach suffers from:

- A human limit of how detailed a pattern each pricing analyst can see and act on.
- Scalability in terms of people-hours required.
- It is not very repeatable—quality and consistency gaps.

On the other hand, a pricing science approach is exactly the opposite:

- It is repeatable and scalable.
- It does not place an additional burden on the Sales team.
- It does not rely on high level rules that won't stay in sync with market conditions.
- It goes one step further in that it allows your company to benefit from demonstrated price sensitivity when it is automatically updating price guidance.

Leaders Must Be Visible and Lead Change

All this 'science-y' stuff will NOT get your company's race car around the course as quickly as you want without some business process changes. As part of any initiative to take a 'science-y' algorithmic approach, it is immensely important to socialize the ideas and the experiences of other companies within your company. There will be nay-sayers and you must win them over with both facts and persuasion.

Frank Ford, an old boss of mine, used to repeatedly say, "Hope is not a method!" If you are asked how a new initiative is going and you utter a phrase like "…we've done X and Y and Z and we hope that will get us over the hump," or something similar, then an alarm bell should go off in your head! If there was nothing more you could do, then you would not still be hoping it will be successful. You would know the outcome!

As a leader, you need to both create the conditions for success and actively manage the message on why this new pricing guidance is in your Sales team's best interests. You need to explain how this new guidance is designed not to replace your Sales Reps or their expertise, but to give them more autonomy to negotiate with confidence in a market-aware price range.

One way to demonstrate your commitment is to implement a new incentive component that rewards the Sales team behavior you want. Traditionally, Sales compensation is based primarily on revenue targets and, to a lesser extent, profit targets. Most companies attempt to measure price realization when they implement some one-size-fits-all price change, and as we have discussed, the stickiness factor is usually in the 1/3 to 2/3's of the price change percent. With market-driven pricing guidance, you can accurately make apple-to-apple comparisons not just on revenue or profit, but also make comparisons on pricing science-based, market-driven, price point attainment. Telling your Sales team they can and will be evaluated on how effectively they use the pricing guidance, and that better use will put more money in their pockets, will help create the conditions for success. (Remember that not all price guidance will go up. Recall the example in Chapter 4: The Big Picture where we said we increased prices in some segments and lowered prices in other segments.)

Your entire Sales team and pricing team needs to clearly hear that this effort leads to greater market agility and to more company profit and more money in their pockets (even without a compensation component change.) You need to sell the ideas behind the new pricing guidance to influential Sales Reps and key managers and engage them in also promoting this change.

Another major part of any new pricing effort is to publicly praise and reward those who support the pricing improvement initiative through their actions. Highlight those who are making great strides and point out those who need help—and get them the help they need to be more effective. This type of visible commitment demonstrates that you can and will measure and reward the desired behavior. Senior executives need to be visibly involved and invested in this new data-driven versus gut-driven pricing approach. They need to be visible champions of this new, innovative approach!

So, how do you **not drive in a blindfold**? In order to be very successful, you must synchronize all your business efforts so that pricing is supportive of what the company has set as market objectives. It is imperative that your company establish a **Pricing Council**. This is **an executive level team to set pricing policy and vision**. This is NOT a tactical team that acts "in pricing", this is a strategic team that acts "on pricing". In most cases, the team members will be at the VP level and above. The Pricing Council will synchronize your pricing team activities with procurement, manufacturing, marketing, product management, sales, and finance. Only through executive action can you support the top and bottom-line business objectives in the market.

Lastly, if YOU want to improve pricing, then YOU must make it happen. The "status quo" parties in your company will not accept that changing how your company approaches pricing can be done with insignificant risk. After all, everyone "knows" that pricing is hard, it's ill-defined, and it's fraught with complexity. There will be late-adopters, and the foot-draggers will want to wait this initiative out.

So, if you want to reap the greatest benefits as quickly as possible, you must engage and lead the change! Changing pricing and improving top-line and bottom-line revenues is a challenge, but it's not impossible. Pricing will get much easier, not harder, when it's rolled out.

Last, be sure to review the references in Appendix 1 to better appreciate the new capabilities pricing science brings!

You Can Do It!

I have some simple questions. I'm no mind reader, but if you have read this far, I bet I know your answers to these questions.

- Do you believe that the same fundamental changes behind improvements in predicting the weather can be leveraged to improve pricing?
- Are you open-minded and willing to believe that there is a strong basis in reality behind the many "pricing science" storylines in many publications over the last 25 years?
- Do you want to improve your top and bottom lines? Do you want to **stop spilling fuel on the track?**
- Do you want to be on the leading edge or the trailing edge in your industry?
- Are you willing to accept that if this pricing 'science-y' algorithmic stuff has been successfully employed in <u>all</u> the below B2B industries, then it can also work in your company?

Distribution	Manufacturing	Services
Apparel Products	Building Products	Cargo Transportation
Automotive Products	Chemicals	Energy
Building Products	Consumer Goods	Equipment Rental
Chemicals & Paint	Electrical Equipment	Facilities
Food & Beverage	Food & Agriculture	Financial
Healthcare Products	Food Ingredients	Healthcare
High-Tech Products	Food Service	Information Storage
Industrial Equipment	Glass, Ceramics & Plastics	Information License
Networking & Telecom	High-Tech	Insurance
Office Supplies	Lighting Products	Logistics
Packaging & Paper	Mill Products	Project
Petroleum	Packaging Products	Other Recurring
Software Products	Paints & Coatings	Uniform & Apparel
Steel & Metals	Petroleum	
	Printing & Paper Products	
	Service/Repair Parts	
	Textiles & Polymers	
	Transportation Products	
	Water Filtration & Treatment	
	Wood & Lumber Products	

The only challenge separating you from creating a more profitable company is your willingness to start on the journey. You just need to decide to start! ***Do it and your company won't be pulling over for more gas while your competitors accelerate around the track!*** Heed Ali Velshi's quote at the beginning of the Introduction.

Appendix 1:
Useful References

The Proof Is In the Patent

US Patent 8,374,906: Filed Sept 30, 2008, and approved Feb 12, 2013
Excerpts from the Abstract and Summary

"To determine pricing recommendations for goods and service products in a business-to-business environment…"

"…embodiments of the present invention utilize a set of transaction data corresponding to a set of products where the pricing recommendation may be optimized according to an objective."

"…embodiments of the present invention may determine a set of segments, associate transaction data with one or more of the segments and formulate a demand model and an associated price elasticity for one or more of the segments based upon the transactions associated with the segment."

"Using these price elasticities, pricing recommendations for each product may be determined for each set of customers and presented to the user."

Pricing References

Listed Chronologically
1. *How Do You Know When the Price is Right*, By Robert J. Dolan in The Harvard Business Review, September-October 1995
   https://hbr.org/1995/09/how-do-you-know-when-the-price-is-right
2. *Revenue Management: Hard Core Tactics for Market Domination* by Robert G. Cross 1997, Crown Business
3. *Pricing and Revenue Optimization* by Robert Phillips 2005, Stanford Business Press
4. *The Art of Pricing* by Rafi Mohammed 2005, Crown Business
5. *The Strategy and Tactics of Pricing* by Tom Nagle/John Hogan 5th edition 2010 ('87/'95/'02/'06), Prentice Hall
6. *The 1% Windfall* by Rafi Mohammed 2010, Harper Business
7. *Smart Pricing* by Jagmohan Ragu/Z John Zhang 2010, Pearson Education
8. *The Price Advantage* by Walter L. Baker/Michael V. Marn/Craig C. Zawada 2010, Wiley Finance
9. *Pricing and Profitability Management* by Julie Meehan/Mike Simonetto/Larry Montan/Chris Goodin 2011, John Wiley
10. *Pricing: Segmentation and Analytics* by Tudor Bodea/Mark Ferguson 2012, Business Expert Press
11. *Higher Profit via Price Optimization* in The Business Owner Journal, April 2012
12. *Price Execution – How to Get Pricing Power into Your Sales Force*, by Harald Schedl, Dr Peter Colman and David Reid, The Journal of Professional Pricing, Vol 21, Number 2, Second Quarter 2012
13. *How Price Execution is Coming of Age*, by Hermann Simon, The Journal of Professional Pricing, Vol 22, Number 1, First Quarter 2013
14. *Pricing: The Third Business Skill, Principles of Price Management*, by Ernst-Jan Bouter 2013, PriceFirst B.V.
15. *Using big data to make better pricing decisions*, McKinsey & Company, Insights and Publications June 2014
16. *Dollarizing Differentiation Value – A Practical Guide for the Quantification and Capture of Customer Value in B2B Markets*, By Stephan M. Liozu, PhD 2016, Value Innoruption Advisors Publishing
17. *The Pricing Model Revolution: How Pricing Will Change the Way We Sell and Buy On and Offline*, By Danilo Zatta, PhD, Wiley

18. *Finding and Leveraging "Hidden" Sources of Margin and Revenue in B2B*, Zilliant Whitepaper

19. HBR Blog: The Benefits of Bargaining with Your Customers, July 2014
    http://blogs.hbr.org/2014/07/the-benefits-of-bargaining-with-your-customers/

20. HBR Blog: The Silent Killer of New Products: Lazy Pricing, Sept 2014
    http://blogs.hbr.org/2014/09/the-silent-killer-of-new-products-lazy-pricing/

21. Professional Pricing Society (PPS) LinkedIn Forum: Price Discount Based On Volume Steps
    Join the PPS LinkedIn Group to access this reference

Non-Pricing References: Stories of How Business Can Leverage Science & Big Data

Listed Chronologically

1. *Competing on Analytics* by Thomas Davenport/Jeanne Harris 2007, Harvard Business School Press
2. *Super Crunchers: Why Thinking-by-Numbers Is the New Way to Be Smart* by Ian Ayres 2008, Bantam Books
3. *The Drunkard's Walk: How Randomness Rules Our Lives* by Leonard Mlodinow 2009, Vintage
4. *Liars Poker* by Michael Lewis 2010, W. W. Norton & Company
5. *The Black Swan* by Nassim Nicholas Taleb 2010, Random House
6. *The Optimization Edge* by Steve Sashihara 2011, McGraw Hill
7. *Money Ball* by Michael Lewis 2011, W. W. Norton & Company
8. *The Quants* by Scott Paterson 2011, Crown Business
9. *Taming The Big Data Tidal Wave* by Bill Franks 2012, John Wiley
10. *The Signal and the Noise* by Nate Silver 2012, Penguin Press
11. *Predictive Analytics* by Eric Siegel/Tom Davenport 2013, John Wiley

Appendix 2:
Glossary of Terms

- Agreement Types
  - *See Pricing Vehicles*
- FILO – First in last out, typically applied to inventory control or service requests. The reverse is LIFO – Last in first out.
- Margin (vs. Profit)
  - For clarity I have adopted the terminology of Profit Dollars = (Price – Cost) versus Margin Rate = (Price – Cost) / Price.
  - I do not use the term Margin Dollars; Profit *means* Dollars and Margin *means* Rate.
- Organization
  - Centralized vs. Decentralized – This refers to the reporting and approval lines for "pricers" not the physical location of the people.
  - Price administrators – Is a generic term that identifies anyone who does not make price setting decisions, but rather administers the agreements and the renewal of those agreements and the entering of orders under those agreements.
  - Pricers – Is a generic term that identifies anyone who makes/negotiates prices in an organization. Such a person could be in the Sales organization, in product management, or in a distinct pricing department.
- Price Elasticity of Demand – How demand changes in response to price changes, or mathematically it is the expected percent change in demand resulting from a one percent change in price.

- Price Segmentation – Segmenting the market along customer, product, and order attributes with the goal of accurately predicting price change response/buying behavior.
- Price Sensitivity – Related to price elasticity but is the amount by which changes in a product's price affect demand for that product. The price sensitivity of a product within its target market is often used by business when determining its optimal pricing and marketing strategy for the product.
- Pricing Strategies
    - Net Price – Is currency denominated pricing, e.g., in USD or Euros, which does not change regardless of cost or List Price or other market changes during the agreed period.
    - Markup (or Markup Value) – Is transaction Net Price divided by transaction cost. The Price to the customer is the Markup times the Cost. As costs rise and fall the Net Price to the customer increases and decreases.
    - List Multiplier – Is transaction price divided by List Price. The Price to the customer is the List Multiplier times the List Price. As List Price rises and falls the Net Price to the customer increases and decreases.
    - Discount From List (or List Down) – Is 1 minus the List Multiplier. The Price to the customer is (1 minus Discount From List) times the List Price. As List Price rises and falls the Net Price to the customer increases and decreases.
    - Maintain Margin (or Margin Float) – Margin Rate = (Price – Cost) / Price. As costs rise and fall, the Net Price to the customer increases and decreases.
    - Margin Float with Ratchet Up – This is different from Maintain Margin in that as costs increase the Price to the customer goes up, but when costs fall the Price to the customer stays the same.
- Pricing Vehicles (aka Pricing Types)
    SEE THE GRAPHIC AT THE END OF THE GLOSSARY
    - "The" List Price vehicle is mostly a positioning statement in the market – most companies would be thrilled to sell to anyone at this price, but they don't expect to sell at this price.
        - "The" List Price (which may also be a catalog or web price) is a special B2B pricing issue in which there is little to nothing known about the customer and there is no price negotiation. In this type of B2B sales opportunity, the requirement is to offer to sell some

product at prices acceptable to a class of unidentified customers which results in a spot or casual transaction.

- Typically, it is set by a central authority and updated infrequently per product.

o The Matrix Price vehicle is often derived from/associated with typical marketing programs employing tiers/buckets/groups associated with price levels. Often businesses use this approach to balance the pricing administration burden and customer value, while also attempting to improve the customer relationship through predictability and stability.

- In the Matrix Price problem, we know who the customer is and what products they are eligible to buy from a matrix price list. Customers are grouped according to affinity or industry or channel or spend or expected spend levels. Sometimes a customer elects to be in a group, other times the company assigns a customer into a tier/bucket/group.

- The Matrix Price is usually calculated via a multiplier applied to a reference price such as the List Price and has many common names such as Column Price, Tier Price or even List Price.

o Negotiated Pricing B2B agreement types:

- Manufacturers that sell via Distributors utilize "Into Stock" or Customer Specific Agreements (CSA) to control product and price availability for different types and sizes of distributors. Distributors hold stock for resale. Generally, the term of the agreement is known but the expected quantity demanded is unknown. The sold-to customer is known but the end user may be unknown.

- Manufacturers also sometimes sell direct to other OEM-type or Distributor customers via "Blanket pricing" agreements (BA) that can apply to one or more customers. If involving a Distributor some refer to this as "rebate up front" pricing since the distributor does not have to claim and substantiate the sales. Under a direct sales agreement with other manufacturers, the buyer does not hold stock for re-sale. Manufacturers may also establish BAs with

"Agents," which do not hold stock for resale, and they functionally serve as non-company commissioned sales brokers.

- Manufacturers sometimes establish "Rebate" agreements or Special Price Agreements (SPA) with distributors to service one or more OEM-type customers or other special customers. The special customer's agreed-to re-sale price may be near or below the distributor's "Into Stock" price. So, the manufacturer pays a rebate to the Distributor to provide the service and "make them whole."

- Spot Market or Project Quote (SQ) or Casual Transactions – When OEM-type customers, distributors or agents become aware of special business opportunities and want to offer more aggressive pricing for a specific bill of materials/parts list, they may request special pricing contingent on the buyer purchasing all (roughly) of the items and quantities defined during some generally defined period.

o The Promotional Pricing vehicle is often attributed to be for some short-term purpose such as "buying market share in Los Angeles for product family Y." But frequently it is just a way to respond to perceived (maybe proven?) competitive pressures over a short time horizon. Often Promotional Pricing is "owned" by a central authority, such as Marketing, and supports a specific market communication plan.

o Price Overrides often come from highly decentralized decision making, varying from one pricing decision to the next. They serve four main purposes: 1) to correct for a perceived mistake in the price list that someone else has carefully set, 2) to correct for some other administrative error, 3) to mitigate a customer relationship issue or 4) to try to "juice" demand through a one-time special offer.

- This last use is often as predictable as the end of the quarter, and hence if used for this reason it often just defers earlier demand or pulls forward later demand and **leaks fuel on the track.**

o The New Product Pricing vehicle is a special case involving market positioning and attempts to reclaim R&D investments early in a product's lifecycle. In many cases this price setting exercise can be a very enhanced and detailed Matrix Pricing exercise involving customer tiers and advanced market analysis using a variety of techniques like adsorption and diffusion analysis. This is not addressed in the scope of this book, but leveraging price segmentation can lead to improved new product price setting activities.

- Stickiness factor – a general rule of thumb on how much of an across-the-board price increase will actually be realized, it depends on the industry, but typically is in the 1/3 to 2/3 range.
- Willingness to Pay – Related to price sensitivity but reflects the largest sum of money an individual is agreeable to pay for a product or service.
- Zone of Indifference – Classically, in any price vs. quantity model a price increase will decrease the demand. In practice we often see cases where small price increases (and decreases) have no impact on the quantity demanded; this narrow range of price indifference is the "Zone of Indifference." For example, if you quoted a price of $988 vs. $987 per case of 5000 widgets it is unlikely this would have any effect on the quantity a customer is expected to buy.

'Pricing Vehicle' Relationships

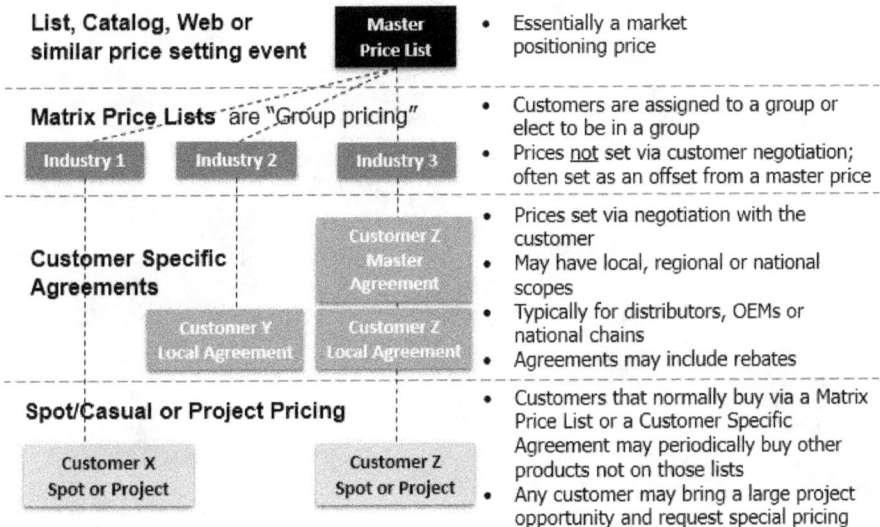

List, Catalog, Web or similar price setting event — Master Price List
- Essentially a market positioning price

Matrix Price Lists are "Group pricing" — Industry 1, Industry 2, Industry 3
- Customers are assigned to a group or elect to be in a group
- Prices not set via customer negotiation; often set as an offset from a master price

Customer Specific Agreements — Customer Z Master Agreement, Customer Y Local Agreement, Customer Z Local Agreement
- Prices set via negotiation with the customer
- May have local, regional or national scopes
- Typically for distributors, OEMs or national chains
- Agreements may include rebates

Spot/Casual or Project Pricing — Customer X Spot or Project, Customer Z Spot or Project
- Customers that normally buy via a Matrix Price List or a Customer Specific Agreement may periodically buy other products not on those lists
- Any customer may bring a large project opportunity and request special pricing

Chart 36 - Visualizing Pricing Vehicle Relationships

End Notes

1. Putting Your Financial House in Order, Ali Velshi, CNN chief business correspondent, July 2009 (link is inactive) http://www.cnn.com/2009/LIVING/01/07/velshi.excerpt.debt/index.htm

2. The motion picture *Rush*, 2013 http://www.imdb.com/title/tt1979320/

3. *Resonate: Present Visual Stories that Transform Audiences* by Nancy Duarte, John Wiley, 2010, pg. 117

4. There are many references on the web and in books to profit leakage and how to address them. A small sampling includes:

   "The Meaning of a Gross Profit Leakage" by Kevin Johnston, Small Business Chronicle http://smallbusiness.chron.com/meaning-gross-profit-leakage-13105.html

   "The Profit Leakage: The Price Waterfall" by Dr. Clemens Oberhammer, CEO Magazine, March 17, 2006

   "Plugging the Profit Leakage — Role of a Price Waterfall" by Stephan A. Butscher, Harshavardhan Ramanan and Clemens Oberhammer, The Pricing Advisor, The Professional Pricing Society, July 2006 (and CEO Journal March 24, 2006)

   "How Profitable are Your Customers … Really", Deloitte Review (link is inactive) http://www.deloitte.com/view/en_US/us/Insights/Browse-by-Content-Type/deloitte-review/18b688c904ea2210VgnVCM200000bb42f00aRCRD.htm

5. *The Art of Pricing* by Rafi Mohammed, 2005, Crown Business

6. Price Elasticity: A Fool's Errand? Started by Jerry Bernstein, The Professional Pricing Society group discussion on LinkedIn, 2012
   JOIN THE PPS LINKEDIN GROUP TO ACCESS THIS REFERENCE

7. *Empirical Model-Building and Response Surfaces* by G.E.P Box and N.R. Draper, 1987, John Wiley and Sons, NY, p 74

8. Modeling the Distribution of Price Sensitivity and Implications for Optimal Retail Pricing by Byung-Do Kim, Robert C. Blattberg, Peter E. Rossi, ASA Journal of Business & Economic Statistics, July 1995; and Using Price Distributions to Estimate Search Costs by Han Hong and Matthew Shum, RAND Journal of Economics, Vol. 37, No. 2, Summer 2006

9. The Power of Pricing in the McKinsey Quarterly, Feb 2003 (link is inactive)
    http://www.mckinsey.com/insights/marketing_sales/the_power_of_pricing
    and *The 1% Windfall* by Rafi Mohammed, 2010, Harper Business

10. Adapted from *Revenue Management: Hard Core Tactics for Market Domination* pg.
    61 by Robert G Cross, and Pricing Your Way to Higher Revenues by Jim
    Vaughn in Atlanta Catalyst Magazine, Nov-Dec 2002, p 50-55

11. "The Profit Leakage: The Price Waterfall" by Dr. Clemens Oberhammer,
    CEO Magazine, March 17, 2006

12. Some of this section is adapted from Profitability: Smart Pricing by Rafe
    VanDenBerg and Barrett Thompson, Manufacturing Today, June 1, 2010

13. Brainy Quotes, April 2014
    http://www.brainyquote.com/quotes/quotes/w/warrenbuff161460.html

14. *Revenue Management: Hard Core Tactics for Market Domination* by Robert G. Cross,
    Crown Business, 1997

15. ibid, Chapter 2, Finding the "Lost" $300 Million

16. "Seven Mistakes of Poor Pricers" by Frank V. Cespedes, Elliot B. Ross and
    Benson P. Shapiro, Wall Street Journal, May 24, 2010

17. "Penny Wise at the NYSE", New York Times, May 15, 2003; and "SEC Aide
    Urges Look at Decimal Trading", Wall Street Journal, May 15, 2003

18. Tutor2u: Profit and Sales Revenue Maximisation Using Marginal Cost and
    Marginal Revenue Curves
    https://www.tutor2u.net/economics/reference/theory-of-the-firm-2021-
    revision-update

19. The Silent Killer of New Products: Lazy Pricing, Sept 2014
    http://blogs.hbr.org/2014/09/the-silent-killer-of-new-products-lazy-pricing

20. Summarized from a Shaw Industries presentation "Getting Started: Enabling
    An Effective B2B Pricing Initiative", September 2010, Las Vegas, NV

21. "CORE Pricing", International Rental News magazine, May 2011, page 54-55

About the Author

Jim Vaughn has worked for over 30 years in the pricing space for both B2C and B2B companies. This work includes consulting with industries and customers ranging from those with $100 million in annual sales to Fortune 100 customers.

Because of his breadth and depth of experience, Jim has a unique perspective on pricing problems that many companies face. He has collected in this book some of his insights from work as a management and pricing consultant, pricing scientist, and pricing product manager. In addition, having held line management responsibilities up to CIO he understands what it means to be the client.

Jim's experience designing and implementing pricing solutions spans a variety of markets and products including airlines, alternate power sources, apartment leasing, broad line distribution, building supplies, chip manufacturing, coatings and paint, commercial and residential lighting, configured parts/assemblies, construction equipment, electrical wiring and motors, food distribution, fuses and circuit protection, glass, hotels, hydraulics and pumps, metals distribution, paper manufacturing, power distribution, rental cars, software licenses, telecommunications, and water filtration.

In addition to his pricing background, Jim spent 28 years in the Army and Army Reserve including work at the Army's Center for Analysis and other Department of Defense executive agencies utilizing his skills as an Operations Research scientist.

Jim's wealth of presentation experience helps him find ways to explain complex technical topics in non-technical, conversational tones to audiences ranging from CXOs to VPs, Directors, Managers, Sales Reps and Pricing Analysts.

Jim currently leads Zilliant's Pricing Consulting Advisory team and is a graduate of the best hands-on leadership program in the world—the US Military Academy at West Point, NY. He also holds an Operations Research Master's Degree from the Georgia Institute of Technology, and he completed additional post-graduate studies in mathematics and leadership at the US Naval Postgraduate School in Monterey, CA and the US Army Command and General Staff College in Leavenworth, KS, respectively.